A ids and
R esearch
T ools in
A ncient
N ear
E astern
S tudies

4

T0156174

JACK M. SASSON

DATED TEXTS FROM MARI: A TABULATION

Undena
Publications

Malibu
1980

AIDS AND RESEARCH TOOLS IN ANCIENT NEAR EASTERN STUDIES

Editor: Giorgio Buccellati

This work offers its users a convenient form by which to locate dated texts from the Old Babylonian Period which have been published in the *Archives Royales de Mari* I-XVIII as well as in various periodicals. In addition, texts which are dated to the same period but were parts of the Chagar Bazar, Tell Ṭaya, and Rimah archives are included.

On individual sheets of 22 x 35.5 cm, dated materials have been entered into spaces of approximately 1 sq. cm. Each one of these squares represents one day of one month of a particular year or eponym. A code has been devised to allow quick evaluation of the type of document entered in each square. To permit easy and quick recovery of each monarch's dated archives, these sheets are printed on different colors. The tabulation sheets are kept unbound in order to allow maximal flexibility in usage. Thus, a reader might juxtapose monthly tabulations horizontally and thereby recover activities in the Mari palace which stretch unbroken over 125 months of Zimri-Lim's reign. Provisions are made for adding information whenever new texts are published. The introduction offers an overview of problems in concerning royal succession, date-formulae and their sequence, and the variety of calendars at use in Mari.

Library of Congress Catalog Card Number: 80-53524
ISBN: 0-8900-3-066-9

PREFACE

Giorgio Buccellati offered a home for this enterprise when he heard of its first plans. Since then, he has been most gracious in accepting the repeated delays which interfered with its completion. At all times, he gave encouragement and suggested practical measures to render this Tabulation as useful as possible to prospective readers. He has my gratitude.

The National Endowment for the Humanities was kind enough to support the initial moments of this enterprise by means of a 1978 Summer Stipend. I am beholden to it.

The work of many Mari specialists made this project possible. But the achievements of the "second generation" of Mari epigraphists, M. Birot, J. Bottéro, M. L. Burke, A. Finet, and J.-R. Kupper, are clearly of signal import to the study of the economic and legal institutions of this Old Babylonian principate. It is to them that this contribution is offered in tribute. I am grateful to M. L. Jaffe for shepherding this material and for compiling Appendix B.

Jack M. Sasson
February 1980

TABLE OF CONTENTS

INTRODUCTION

1. Materials

1.1 This fascicle offers its users a convenient form by which to locate dated texts in the Mari archives.

1.1.1 The listings are culled from the documents published in ARM[T] I-XIV, XVIII, to which were also added allusions to dated texts which have been made in articles, reviews, and, in a few cases when permission was granted, private communications. No information that reached me after December 1979 was entered.

1.1.2 The entries do not include materials which are assignable to the *šakkanakku* periods or, for that matter, those preceding the reign of Yaḫdun-Lim of Mari.

1.2 **Documents from outside Mari.** Because other OB documents have produced dated texts which parallel those from Mari, I have incorporated the data from the following sites:

1.2.1 **Chagar Bazar.** I have distinguished between the British Museum holdings, published by O. Loretz, AOAT 3/1 (1969) [cf. *Lišan mitḫurti*, AOAT 1 (1969), 244-260] and those, uncopied as yet, still found in Aleppo, by underlining the letters CB preceding the text number [*CB*]. For the Aleppo texts, I relied on the catalogues of Gadd, *Iraq* 4(1937), 178-185; 7(1940), 22-66. The opinions of the reviewers of Loretz's edition have been taken into consideration (cf. Borger, HKL, II, 187).

1.2.2 **Rimah.** One text from Rimah, [Dalley, *et. al.*, *The OB Tablets from Rimah*, 1976], No. 314, has been incorporated. Birot's review of that volume, RA 62(1978), 181-190, is especially helpful in clarifying the connections between Mari and Rimah.

1.2.3 **Tell Ṭaya.** One text from that site has been entered (cf. *Iraq* 35(1973), 125).

1.2.4 The inscription attributed to Šamši-Adad, RA 7(1909), 151-156 [Grayson, ARI, 1,155-158], has been taken into account, even if the precise year in which its activities occurred is yet a matter of speculation.

1.2.5 It is hoped that, as more documents are found, the blank spaces will be filled by the users.

2. Presentation

2.1 On 8.5" x 14" [22 x 35.5 cm.] pages, dated materials have been entered into spaces of about 1 square centimeter. Each one of these squares represents one day of one month of a particular year or eponym.

2.1.1 In most cases, a square would contain reference to one dated text. In the lower left hand corner of that square, a code is given to indicate the nature of the text in question. For the code, see below, at 2.4.

2.1.2 When more than one text is dated to the same day, and hence must occupy the same box, the information is simply stacked, one reference above the other. For the layout of the code, however, see below, 2.4.1.2-4.

2.1.3 Because conditions can be crowded in certain cases, most often when more than three references occupy the same space, the data is placed in the square immediately above. Two notations indicate when this approach is at stake. *a.* An arrow pointing downward, is placed alongside such entries and *b.*The perimeters of the square thus used is heavily lined, except for the bottom part which is totally erased.

2.2 **Long term accounts.** Whenever monthly accounts, or any other account, stretches over many days, only the *first day of that account is entered.* A black line, spanning the period covered by the document, is begun from that first day; the last day within that account is indicated by the fact that the line ends at that point with an arrow point (——→).

2.2.1 In cases when breaks are found within a monthly account or register, since the purpose of this fascicle is to indicate the occurrence of *dated information*, the pattern described in 2.2 is repeated. This obtains even when we are certain that the break involved specific dates.

2.3 **Difficult readings or suggested completion of dates.** A text which allows two or more readings of an individual date, whether it concerns a day, month or date-year eponym, is repeated as often as necessary. The various possibilities are given, however, between brackets. A certain amount of subjectivity enters each and every decision that pertains to this condition.

2.3.1 A text which has been corrected, either because of improved reading, collation, and/or because of a convincing opinion by various scholars, is entered into our list in its improved form and not in that which obtains in the ARM[T] series. An exclamation point (!) is placed, usually, alongside. I regret that it is not possible to offer the user precise literature on such corrections.

2.3.2 J.M. Durand, assisted by D. Charpin, has collated ARM[T] VIII. Their readings, to appear in *Cahiers de Mari,* 1 (= *Syria* 57) 1980, have been kindly placed at my disposal. I have indicated their readings by placing a c. ["collated"] in proximity to the (corrected) reference.

2.3.3 A number of monthly accounts, which do not normally bear date-years, can be assigned to specific years on the basis of daily accounts [cf. Birot, ARMT XII, p. 15; Sasson, *Festschrift Kraus*, forthcoming]. I have done so in those cases which are certain. In others, I have either kept them at the bottom of the page, with the incomplete entries (cf. 2.3.4), or placed them, *bracketed*, in a specific year.

2.3.4 Texts that bear incomplete dates are reserved to the last three horizontal registers: *a.* Unknown Year; *b.* Unknown Year/Day; *c.* Unknown Day. It should be obvious that the last two horizontals, because the day in question is unavailable, register the entries in no specific sequence. The last horizontal, however, which takes into account texts in which only the month name is missing, incorporates the year-date / eponym which is at stake.

2.3.5 On separate pages, I have also given those texts which cannot be placed in our lists because the month at stake is not available (below, 6.0.0).

2.4 **Code.** In order to allow quick overview of the contents of a text entered in our tables, I have devised a code and placed it at the lower left hand corner of each square. *This code is highly simplistic and is meant to be only suggestive.* It is hoped, however, that this system would allow a quick overview of the data at hand.

2.4.1 The *arrangement* of this code follows this pattern:

2.4.1.1 In case of a single entry, the code is placed in the lower left hand corner.

2.4.1.2 In case of multiple entries, the *lower right hand corner* is given over to the *second reference*, i.e. the one which appears below the first. The *middle space* at the code line is reserved for the *third reference.*

2.4.1.3 For references that spill over the square above [cf. 2.1.3], the pattern for coding is repeated.

2.4.1.4 Codes for monthly accounts, or for those which register sequences that stretch over a number of days, are placed in their proper spacing normally for the first day of entry only. When space permits, however, and *especially if changes occur in the contents of such accounts*, the code is repeated or changed to alert the users to these peculiarities.

2.4.2 The abbreviations represent the following types of text:

A: ADMINISTRATIVE

/f: food outlay (*not* including the *naptan šarrim* food expenditures)

/m: messengers

/p: personnel

/o: oil for annointing

/s: oil for annointing the king

E: EPISTOLARY

/tx: taxing for shipping [mostly concerns ARMT XIII:58-101]

F: FOOD OUTLAYS [mostly *naptan šarrim* (NÍG.DU/NÌ.GUB LUGAL)]

/o: oil for the royal meal

/m: meals taken at Mari

/s: "Soldiers (*ṣābum*)" joining the meal

/t(r): meal taken while away from Mari

/tx: taxes related to foodstuff

/x: meals taken on special circumstances

[N.B.: F/R meals taken during religious activities.]

L: /l: loan

/t(x): taxes

R: RELIGIOUS

/k: *kispum* ceremonies (includes other funerary activities)

/p: annointing during religious ceremonies.

2.4.2.1 In some cases, I have used combinations of the above codes in order to give a more precise indication on the content of texts.

3. Dating

3.1 **Date-Years and Eponyms.** The basic listing of date-years and eponyms is Dossin's presentation in *Studia Mariana* (1950), 51-61. Our entries give an abbreviated form of the date-years, followed, between parentheses, by the number assigned by Dossin. This number will allow the users to return to Dossin's pages for full forms of each date-year and for variations on each of these forms.

3.1.1 In our own citations of date formulae, we have followed the syntax that is suggested by Horsnell, JNES 36(1977), 277-285.

3.1.2 VIII:46 contains fragments of a year-date which cannot be allocated to any Mari ruler.

3.2 **Rulers mentioned in the Mari texts.**

3.2.1 **Yaḫdu(n)-Lim** (Dossin, *St. Mar.*, p. 52).

3.2.1.1 There is a good chance that #2 (Zalma[. . .]) and #3 (Zalpaḫ) are but variations of the same formula.

3.2.1.2 Anbar, *Israel Oriental Studies*, 3(1973), 6, suggests that #5 (ZAB[· · ·]) is to be completed as follows: "Year: Yaḫdu-Lim defeated Benjaminite troops in Terqa."

3.2.1.3 VIII:75 gives: "Year: Yaḫdu-Lim defeated the Benjaminites." Durand's collation of VIII:51 can conceivably permit the reading of the same formula, with "Benjaminites" given in the genitive. This year has been listed by me as "Benjaminites."

Anbar, *Is. Or. St.* 3(1973), 7, might be right in suggesting that #5 and this formula are the same. For the sake of prudence, I have kept them separate.

3.2.1.4 Equivalence between #5, the formulae attested in VIII:75; 51, and #6 ["Year: Yaḫdu-Lim went to Ḫen and controlled the settlements of the Benjaminites"] is to be kept as a possibility.

3.2.1.5 VIII:61 offers a formula not collected by Dossin: "Year: The one following that in which Yaḫdu-Lim [built? (cf. Durand's collation)] the temple of Šamaš."

3.2.1.6 Another year-name for Yaḫdun-Lim has been reported by Dossin, RA 61(1967), 20: "Year: Yaḫdu-Lim defeated Šamši-Adad at the gate of Nagar."

3.2.2 **Sumu-Yamam** (Dossin, *St. Mar.*, 52-53).

On the order of kingship among Mari's rulers, see, with previous suggestions, Anbar, *Is. Or. St.* 3(1973), 7-10.

3.2.2.1 A second year named after #9 ["Year: Sumu-Yamam built Saggaratum's ramparts."] has been repeatedly attested in the archives published by Dossin, RA 64(1970), 17-43. On this year-formula, see further, below, 4.4.2.

3.2.2.2 It should be noted that documents published in the above-mentioned article are entered in our tabulation by *text number*, and not by the page in which each text occurs.

3.2.3 **Šamši-Adad** (Dossin, *St. Mar.*, 53).

3.2.3.1 A rereading of the first formula, after collation by Dossin, is given in Kupper, *Nomades en Mesopotamie*, p. 54, n. 1: "Year: Šamši-Adad captured DUMU-Addu, and built the temple of Dagan."

3.2.3.2 In a note in ARMT VIII to the formula of text #43 (p. 67, n. 3), Boyer suggests that Šamši-Adad's date-year #2 ["Year: Šamši-Adad piled up the earthen ramparts of Šubat-Šamaš."] may have to be repeated. Durand's collation confirms that this is not the case. It is my suggestion that Dossin's own reading of this year-name in *St. Mar.* is, in fact, based precisely on VIII:43 and that its beginning should read MU.1.KAM rather than Dossin's [*šar*]*rum* (?). For the sake of prudence, however, I have kept two spots for this year-name.

3.2.3.3 VIII:45 suggests a year name not listed by Dossin. Durand's collation confirms the possibility of reading: "Year: Šamši-Adad [. . . kin]g of Mari." [See also VIII:46.]

3.2.4 **Yasmaḫ-Adad** (Dossin, *St. Mar.* 53-54).

3.2.4.1 Two year formulae and 17 eponyms are associated with Yasmaḫ-Adad. In the case of #3 (Eponym: "Addu-bani"; "Year: The census was taken in the land."), where the two are equated by the chancery, it has been suggested that this reflects a transition in the regimes of the "Lim" and "Assyrian" dynasties, cf. Landsberger, JCS 8 (1954), 35. Anbar, *Is. Or. St.* 3(1973), 17-18, thinks that the Šamši-Adad years entertained above (3.2.3.0) follow this eponym/date-year.

3.2.4.2 It has been suggested that the eponym Ṭāb-ṣilli-Ašur II (#17) may have been the last to witness Yasmaḫ-Adad's reign at Mari; Larsen RA 68 (1974), 19-20; Sasson, *Studies . . . Tom B. Jones* [AOAT 203, 1979], 122.

3.2.5 **Išar-Lim** (Dossin, *St. Mar.* 53).

3.2.5.1 Until documents are published which bear the only date-year cited by Dossin ["Year: Išar-Lim entered kingship."], there will only be speculations concerning this enigmatic figure. He is likely to have been a provincial ruler. Discussions can be had in Finet, AIPHOS 15(1958-1960), 31-32; Anbar, *Is. Or. St.* 3(1973), 21. See also the listings in ARM XVI/1, 128, 1°; 2°.

3.2.6 **Zimri-Lim** (Dossin, *St. Mar.*, 54-59).

Dossin offers 32 date-formulae, some of which show variations in formulation and spelling. Birot's recent article, *Syria* 55(1978), 333-343 is fundamental in reorganizing the sequence of a large number of these date-years. In our tabulations for this king's reign, we have devoted the first page to the sequence offered by Birot (see below, 5., for reasons). The remaining pages follow the listing of Dossin minus those formulae that have been placed on the first page. We have retained, between parentheses, the numbering scheme proposed by Dossin.

3.2.6.1 A number of new formulae and changes in those previously listed by Dossin are to be noted:

3.2.6.1.1 XI:149 gives a "2nd year" for "Ḫatta" (#21).

3.2.6.1.2 A MU.EGIR (=? "2nd year") for 'Kaḫat' (#4) has been noted by Birot, *op. cit.*, 333 and 343 n. 2a. It has been entered as 'Kaḫat II' in our listing.

3.2.6.1.3 Durand has communicated to Birot, *op. cit.*, 343, n. 2a, a "second year" for 'Census' (#26). It has been placed in our tabulation as the last listing on p. 3.

3.2.6.1.4 A slightly different formula for #32 has been given by Birot, *op. cit.*, p. 334.

3.2.6.1.5 A heretofore unattested year formula, and variation on it, is reported by Birot, *ibid*: "Year: Z.L. besieged Andariq". We have entered it as (#33!).

3.2.6.2 While awaiting a new year-date to be formulated (cf. XIII:27; 47), the ZL chancery would use the old formula under the rubric MU.2.KAM, MU.MÌN, and, according to Birot, MU.EGIR. In our listings we give such expressions the designation "xxx II." It is not unknown that even when a new formulation has been issued by the central administration, the "second year" usage is continued. In one case, the year "Benjaminites II" (#7), was kept up even into the 8th month. In no case, so far, however, could we show that the scribe *recopied* or *redated* texts, assigned temporarily to "second year" formulation, when a new date year was issued. This might reinforce our opinion, expressed in the *Festschrift Kraus* (forthcoming), that very few of these texts were ever consulted again.

3.2.6.3 Texts are also known in which Zimri-Lim is recorded as having done a certain act a "second time," *šaniš*. These are not likely to be a variation of the formulation for the above, and should be considered as original-date-year. We have regarded a few of these, involving 'Ašlakka' (#3) and 'Babylon' (#12), as such, and have distinguished them from the "second year" dating by calling them "IInd xxx."

3.2.6.4 Birot, in the article cited above, has shown that 18 (actually 19, cf. p. 343, n. 2a) year formulae listed by Dossin can be collapsed and sequenced into a dozen actual years (cf. pp. 341-342). We have followed his proposal and, as stated above, placed that sequence on the first page of the ZL tabulation. We were obliged, however, to retain slots for the "second year" formulation, in order to give access to texts which are not repeated in the 'actual' year that follows.

Thus the series of sequenced ZL years reads as follows:

	"Year after"	"Actual year"
1.		Euphrates (#29)
2.		Benjaminites (#6)
3.	Benjaminites II (#6)	Ašlakka (#2)
4.	Ašlakka II (#3)	Throne of Šamaš (#16)
5.	Throne of Šamaš II (#17)	Census (#26)
6.	Census II (#26b)	Dūr Yaḫdun-Lim (#28)
7.		Hatta (#21)
8.	Ḫatta II (21b)	Elam Expedition (#13)
9.		Addu of Mahanum (#18)
10.		Babylon (#11)
11.	Babylon II (#12)	Throne of Dagan (#14)
12.	Throne of Dagan (#15)	IInd Ašlakka (#3b)

I have retained "IInd Ašlakka" (#3b) in the sequence given by Birot although I have reservations about its location.

3.2.6.5 Although this may not be the place to entertain the relationship between ZL's date-years and the actual number of years he ruled at Mari, a few remarks might yet be in order. The issue has been a vexed one ever since Dossin's listing was made available in *Studia Mariana.* Even if one takes into account the "second year" formulae, we are still left with a number of years that defy synchronism with those of Hammurabi of Babylon (see below). We might, as did Röllig, XVe RAI, 1967, 98, regard the two formulae given as numbers 8 and 9 as but variations of #9 (read: *e-la-aḫ!-tim* in 8). We might, even if quite hazardously, question the individuality of the "second time" formulae. Even with these measures, we still have to contend with 27 years of rule for ZL.

Birot, *op. cit.*, 337, brings arguments to bear that the year "Throne of Dagan" (14) is coeval with Hammurabi's 30th year. The discussion would remain open, however, concerning the ZL date-formulae which were in use between Hammurabi 30 and 32 or 34—whichever, one feels, was the one which saw ZL's demise. I would certainly place the following into contention: "IInd Ašklakka" (#3b), "IInd Babylon" (#12b)—even if it may seem inconceivable that ZL would be aiding Hammurabi at this late stage of his career—; "Mubalittum" (#31); "Kaḫat I and II" (4, 4b; cf. 3.2.6.1.2) [on the sequence of these years and their relatively late position in ZL date formulae, see Birot, RA 66(1972), 137].

The beginning of ZL's reign is usually considered to begin with Yasmaḫ-Adad's expulsion, calculated either to match the year of Šamši-Adad's death, generally placed at Hammurabi 10 or 12, or four years later when Ibal-pī-El of Ešnunna conquered Rapiqum (cf. Kupper, CAH^{2}, II/I (1963), 9-10; H. Lewy, WdOr. 2(1959), 445-453). Arguments have been offered which would account for all of Zimri-Lim's date-years within the period sandwiched, maximally, between Hammurabi 10-34; minimally between 16-32. It has been suggested that ZL began his reign in another city-state and brought his archives along when he ousted Yasmaḫ-Adad [S. Smith, RSO 32(1957), 159ff]. Others have suggested that he remained on the throne well into Samsu-iluna's reign (H. Lewy, XVe RAI (1967), 25-26; Rowton, CAH^{2}, I/6, (1962), 41). With little evidence to support these contentions, scholars have met them with little enthusiasm.

The great number of date-years notwithstanding, it is observable that the bureaucratic and legal documentation have yielded only about a dozen or so year-names (and this includes the "second year" and "year after" formulae) which accommodate about 90% of the documentations. Birot's article has indicated that only about a dozen years or so can be properly placed in sequence. Under these circumstances, I am emboldened, without adequate proofs however, to suggest that Zimri-Lim did not reign more than 18-20 years. Thus, if he were defeated and ousted in Hammurabi 32/34, he probably did not replace Yasmaḫ-Adad much before Hammurabi 14 or so. And I would propose that many of the formulae that have found little attestations so far—and this *might* include years entered into Birot's sequence such as "Addu of Maḫanum" (#18)—were local or provincial equivalents to the better attested ones. In this respect, note that the 9th formula ("Elaḫtum") has so far been attested only at Dēr (RA 66(1972), 135) and at Terqa (IX:13; cf. Birot, ARMT IX, 267; cf. p. 249, §8). Further, note that the year-dates "Addad of Appan II" (#24), "Digging of the Ḫabur" (#30), and "Yamḫad" (#32) have so far been used only in temple loan contracts.

3.2.6.6 In cases involving a loan document which is dated to a year whose sequence is known to us, I have entered the due date for the month of Abum in the year *following* that in which the contract was issued.

4. Menology [discussion in Limet, ARMT XIX, 10-14].

4.1 **Zimri-Lim.** In completing this section, it might be more appropriate to begin with the Zimri-Lim calendar.

4.1.1 The sequence of months during the ZL period, first deduced by Birot, ARMT XII, 20-22, has been confirmed by Kupper on the basis of an unpublished register from room 135 (*Symbolae...de Liagre Böhl*, 1973), 226-270. We have placed a Roman numeral before each month's name, in order to indicate the position of each month within that sequence. We repeat this listing here, for convenience's sake:

I. Urāḫum
II. Malkānum
III. Laḫḫum
IV. Abum
V. Ḫibirtum
VI. IGI.KUR
VII. Kinūnum
VIII. Dagan
IX. Liliatum
X. Bēlet-bīri
XI. Kiskissum
XII. Ebūrum.

4.1.2 **Intercalation.** [Cf. Larsen, RA 68(1974), 17-18; Sasson, *Studies. . .Tom B. Jones* (AOAT, 203) 121]. During the ZL period, two slots appear to have been set aside for intercalation: 1. before the 6th month (IGI.KUR), a Ḫibirtum II was inserted; it can also be considered that this intercalation occurred right after the regular month of Ḫibirtum. 2. After the last month of Ebūrum the year was extended by means of an Ebūrum II.

4.1.2.1 Thanks to the sequence of date years which has been established by Birot, we can note that between the years 'Benjaminites' (#6) and 'Throne of Dagan' (#14), a period which stretches over 10 years, the chancery resorted to intercalation 3 times. An Ebūrum II "elongated" the year 'Benjaminites' (#6). More noteworthy, however, is the apparent insertion of a Ḫibirtum II in each one of *two consecutive years*: 'Babylon' (#11) and 'Throne of Dagan' (#14). This last would confirm the fact that intercalation at Mari was arrived at on an *ad hoc* basis.

4.1.3 A few documents are dated after non-Mari calendars. P/Birizarru appears to be a Terqa month. According to Durand's collation, Adnatum seems to have been used in Carchemish (*sic*, rather than Karsum).

4.1.3.1 Von Soden, AHw 1382b, suggests that the month of Ṭebētum is to be found in II:62:14. Because the context is fragmentary, we have not taken this month name into account.

4.1.3.2 A number of month names associated with ZL's epistolary archives have not been assigned individual tabulating sheets.

a. KUR, to be related most likely to the month name of the *šakkanakku* period, ^{d}KUR, occurs in a letter of Ibal-pī-El; Thureau-Dangin, RA 33(1936), 175:37. It is not clear to me how Birot's suggestion, to read ITI.KAM rather than ITI KUR, mentioned in XVI/1, 271, fits the context of this letter.

b. ITI *i-bi-ib*[. . .], which for no clear reason CAD I/J, p. 2, treats under the unique attestation *Ibibtum*, occurs in an excerpt of a letter sent to ZL. It may be that Ebirtu (i.e. Ḫibirtum) is to be read here.

4.2 **Išar-Lim.** No significant data available as yet.

4.3 **"Assyrian" period.** During this period, two calendars are attested in the Mari archives. This case obtains even when documents can be shown to have originated, and not merely stored, at Mari.

4.3.1 The so-called 'Mari' calendar, known from the ZL period and described above (4.1 ff.), is available in all its months.

4.3.1.1 It is noteworthy that the eponym 'Ṭāb-ṣilli-Ašur' II (#12), considered by some to reflect dated documentations from Yasmaḫ-Adad's last year at Mari, is attestable as far as the 25th day of the 9th month (Liliatum).

4.3.2 Another calendar is similar to ones found in Rimah, Chagar Bazar, and on occasions, in the Diyala region. A bibliography on this calendar includes: Pomponio, *OrAnt.* 16(1977), 333-335; Anbar, *Is. Or. St.* 3(1973), 26-27; Larsen, RA 68(1974), 16-21. A list of months in this calendar is given below. Those that occur only in the "Assyrian" period are preceded by an asterisk (*). A code is given to indicate that our evidence, preserved in the *Mari* archives, is restricted to a specific type of document.

1.	*Mana	E, Ao/R
2.	*Ayārum	E, [L], Ao/R
3.	*Maqrānum	E, Ao/R
4.	*Dumuzi	E [cf. XVI/1, 273]
5.	Abum	E
6.	*Tīrum	E, [A]
7.	Kinūnum	
8.	*Mammītum	E, Ao, R, L
9.	Niqmum	E
10.	*Tamḫīrum	E, L, A
11.	Nabrû	[Chagar Bazar]
12.	*Addaru [ŠE.KIN.KUD]	E; [*kispum* for Sargon and Naram-Sin for this month; Birot, RAI, Copenhagen.]

4.3.2.1 Larsen, RA 68(1974), 17 proposes a synchronism between the 'Mari' and "Assyrian" calendars:
Urāḫum ≘ Mammītum; Malkānum ≘ Niqmum, etc. . .

4.3.3 One intercalary month, DIRIG.GA, is attested in Šamši-Adad's correspondence (I:70). In Larsen's scheme, this would follow Addaru and hence would be equivalent, in position, to Ḫibirtum II.

4.3.4 The (Terqa) month P/Birizarru (spelling *bi-ri!-za-ri-im* in VIII:40 is collated by Durand) occurs in the Yasmaḫ-Adad date-year (*sic*) "Nergal," *St. Mar.* p. 53 (#3).

4.4 **Sumu-Yamam.** [Limet, ARMT XIX, p. 11].

4.4.1 The calendar used by the Sumu-Yamam scribe appears to be the 'Mari' prototype. As of now, we have, however, attestations only on the months of Urāḫum, IGI.KUR, Liliatum, Bēlet-bīri, and Ebūrum II (intercalary). Waraḫsamnu (APIN.DU$_8$), also appearing during that period, may itself be a substitute for (??) Kinūnum (cf. CAD A/2, 221; Von Soden, OLZ 67(1972), 348-349).

Kupper, *Symbolae . . . de Liagre Böhl*, 267-268, n. 6, refers to the attestations of Malkānum and Ḫibirtum in as yet unpublished Sumu-Yamam texts.

4.4.2 A most interesting aspect of Sumu-Yamam's archives is the occurrence of a large number of texts dated to the first half of the intercalary month Ebūrum II *during the date-formula 'Saggaratum' II.* Such an occurrence can indicate that the following conditions may be at stake:

a. The chancery never replaced the date-year 'Saggaratum' II by means of a new formulation, even as late as the 13th month of that year. However, the fact that we have no other texts previous to Ebūrum II, may indicate that another factor is to be considered.

b. Rather than locating Ebūrum II at the end of the year 'Saggaratum', the chancery bought time by locating it as the *opening month* of a temporary, used for only a short time, 'Saggaratum' II. In other words, *this intercalation is regarded as preceding a new year*, rather than ending an old one.

4.4.2.1 In this regard, correct Dossin's translation of a Sumu-Yamam text, #29:12, by striking out his "(qui a suivi)" from RA 65(1970), 37].

4.5 Yaḫdu(n)-Lim. The attested month names from this period, Laḫḫum (#3), Abum (#4), Dagan (#8), and Kiskissum (#11), indicate that the calendar better known to us from the reign of ZL was used.

5. Suggested Usage

This fascicle has kept the calendar tabulations unbound in order to permit maximal flexibility in usage. In turning to the ZL tabulations, for example, one might sequence the individual sheets as follows:

a. *Horizontally.* Because we are now able to locate about a dozen years of ZL's reign in a specific sequence, and because we know the order of the months, as well as the precise location of intercalary expansions, juxtaposing each monthly tabulation would permit us an almost unmatched reconstruction of palace activities which would range for approximately 125 months.

b. *Vertically.* This would allow us to ascertain whether or not certain palace activities occurred in a fixed position in a given month of differing years, regardless of correspondence with the solar cycle.

5.1 It remains to be said that, because errors can easily creep into a work of this nature, users are urged to check into the original documentations before drawing conclusions. Corrections to this tabulation will be gratefully accepted.

5.2 At the end of each ruler's tabulation, I have included blank sheets, easily reproducible, in order to permit registration of materials that do not fit the present format, and to allow recording of as yet unattested calendars.

6. APPENDIX A: Texts with Missing or Unrecorded Months

The following list gives the texts in the Mari Archives which are not entered in the tabulations by month (i.e. for which the months are either broken or missing).

	Text	Category	Year	Day
I.	Yaḫdun-Lim			
	VIII:57?			
II.	Sumu-Yamam			
	VIII:2	L		
	VIII:3	L		
	VIII:63	L	Ḫalabit	
	VIII:101?	Ll		
	RA 64, 3	A	Saggaratum [II?]	
	RA 64, 13	A	Saggaratum	
III.	Yasmaḫ-Adad			
	VIII:8	L	Addu-bani/Census	
	VIII:11	L	DUMU-Addu	
	CBA.997	A	Nemer-Sin	
IV.	Šamši-Adad			
	VIII:43	LI	Šubat-Šamaš [collated]	
	VIII:45	LI	Mari [collated]	
V.	Zimri-Lim			
	VII:88	A	Benjaminite	25 [cf. **XII**, p. 20, n. 2]
	VII:90	A	Babylon I	
	VII:100	A	Dagan	
	VII:104	A	Throne of Šamaš I	14, 17
	VII:123	A	Ḫatta?	
	VII:140	A	Census	
	VII:176	A	Dūr Yaḫdun-Lim	
	VII:177	A	Dūr Yaḫdun-Lim	
	VII:180-196	Ap		
	VII:198-203	Ap		
	VII:199	A		
	VII:205-206	A		
	VII:207	A		24-26
	VII:210-216	Ap		
	VII:218	A		
	VII:219	A		1-6, 20
	VII:220-223	A		
	VII:224	R		
	VII:227	A		
	VII:229	A		
	VII:231-236	A		
	VII:238-254	A		
	VII:255	A		

Text	Category	Year	Day
VII:256-257	F/A		
VII:260, 261	A		
VII:263-265	A		
VII:266	Ap		
VII:268	Ap		
VII:269	F/A		
VII:270	A		
VII:271	F/A		
VII:272-273	A		
VII:275	Ap		
VII:276	A		
VII:277	A		
VII:277-279	Mathem?		
VII:280	Ap		
VII:285	A	Census	
VII:287	A		
VII:288-289	Ap		
VII:290-292	A		
VII:293-296	A		
VII:299-300	?		
VII:302	?		
VII:304-307, 309	Ap		20+
VIII:30	Ll	Yamḫad	
VIII:41	Ll		
VIII:44	Ll		
VIII:53	Ll		
VIII:64	L		
VIII:67	L		
VIII:72 (cf.31)	L		
VIII:76	L		
VIII:84 (cf. 16)	L		
VIII:85	L		
VIII:92	Ll		
VIII:99			21
IX:45	Ap	Throne of Šamaš	1
IX:129	A	Census	
IX:130	F	Census	
IX:192	Fo	Dūr Yaḫdun-Lim	
IX:202	F		
IX:205	Rk		
IX:207	Fs		
IX:208	F		17
IX:209	F	[Ḫatta?]	
IX:235	Fo		9
IX:238,239	F/A		
IX:259	A		
IX:272	Ap		
IX:274,275	A		
IX:278,279	A		
IX:283	A		
IX:284	A/R [cf. CAD K, 92(a,1)]		
IX:285,296	A/p		
IX:297	Seal		
IX:298	A/p		

Text	Category	Year	Day
IX:299-300	Math		
XI:46,47	Fms	Benjaminite	
XI:109,110	FM/s	Throne of Šamaš	
XI:111	Fo	Throne of Šamaš	
XI:147,148	F	Ḫatta	
XI:196	F	Census	
XI:253-254	F	Dūr Yaḫdun-Lim	
XI:289-291	F		
XI:292	Fc		
XI:293	F		
XI:294	A		
XI:295-300			
XII:136	F	Elam Expedition	
XII:260-262	Fms	Throne of Šamaš	
XII:263	Fc	Throne of Šamaš [Kiskissum-Bēlet Bīri]	
XII:359	F	Ḫatta	
XII:360	Fo	Ḫatta	12
XII:469	F	Census	
XII:470	Fo	Census	
XII:471,472	F/R?	Census	
XII:608	Fc	Dūr Yaḫdun-Lim	
XII:609-610	F	Dūr Yaḫdun-Lim	
XII:611	Fc	Dūr Yaḫdun-Lim	
XII:612	Fc	Dūr Yaḫdun-Lim	
XII:613	A	Dūr Yaḫdun-Lim	
XII:614	Rk/o	Dūr Yaḫdun-Lim	
XII:615	Fo	Dūr Yaḫdun-Lim	
XII:651	Fm		
XII:652-656	F		
XII:682	Rk		
XII:683,684	F		
XII:685,686	F?		
XII:687			
XII:695	memo		
XII:695-699	Fc		30 [#699]
XII:710,711	Fo/c		
XII:712,713	Fc		
XII:714,715	Fm		
XII:726	Fo		
XII:728	F/A		
XII:739	F/A		
XII:740	A		
XII:742-745	A		
XII:747	F/p		1, 28-30
XIII:27;47	E	Babylon I/II	
RA 64,99-100	A		
S. 160:3 [ARMT XVIII, 109]	A	Banks of the Euphrates	
S. 160:20 [ARMT XVIII, 109]	A/p		
S. 160:231 [ARMT XVIII, 109]			

The following texts cannot be attributed to a specific ruler.

Text	Category	Year	Day
VIII:5	L	Census/ -	
VIII·35	L1		
VIII:38	L1		
VIII:46	L1		
VIII:83	A		
VIII:95,96	Ap		
VIII:100	Fc		
VIII:101		- /Warahsamna	9/19/29 [collated]

APPENDIX B. Summary Tabulation of Dates by Years and Months (by M. L. Jaffe)

	I URĀḪUM	II MALKĀNUM	III LAḪḪUM	IV ABUM	V ḪIBIRTUM	VI IGI.KUR	VII KINŪNUM	VIII DAGAN	IX LILIATUM	X BĒLET-BĪRI	XI KISKISSUM	XII EBŪRUM	II EBŪRUM (Intercalary)	WARAḪSUMNU
YAḪDUN-LIM														
Paḫudar (1)	–	–	–	–	–	–	–	–	–	–	–	–	–	–
Zalma (2)	–	–	–	–	–	–	–	–	–	–	–	–	–	–
Zalpaḫ (3)	–	–	–	4	–	–	–	–	–	–	–	–	–	–
Imar (4)	–	–	–	–	–	–	–	–	–	–	–	–	–	–
Zab [ ] (5)	–	–	–	–	–	–	–	–	–	–	–	–	–	–
Ḫen/Benjaminites (6)	–	–	15	–	–	–	–	–	–	–	–	–	–	–
Šamši-Addu (7)	–	–	–	–	–	–	–	–	–	–	–	–	–	–
Šamaš	–	–	–	–	–	–	–	–	–	–	–	–	–	–
Šamaš II	–	–	–	15	–	–	–	–	–	–	–	–	–	–
Benjaminites	–	–	–	–	–	–	–	–	–	–	–	–	–	–
Nagar	–	–	–	–	–	–	–	–	–	–	–	–	–	–
Unknown year	–	–	20	–	–	–	–	–	–	–	–	–	–	–
Unknown year & day	–	–	–	–	–	–	–	–	–	–	–	–	–	–
Unknown day	–	–	–	–	–	–	–	1	–	–	1,29	–	–	–
Išar-Lim kingship	–	–	–	–	–	–	–	–	–	–	–	–	–	–
SUMU-YAMAM														
Ḫalabit	9,19 29	–	–	–	–	9	–	3	–	5	–	–	8	15,29
Saggaratum	–	–	–	–	–	–	–	15	9	–	–	–	–	–
Saggaratum II	–	–	–	–	–	–	–	–	–	–	–	–	1,2+	–
Unknown year	–	–	–	–	–	–	–	–	15	–	–	–	–	–
Unknown year & day	–	1	–	–	1	–	–	–	–	–	–	–	1	–
Unknown day	–	–	–	–	–	–	–	–	–	–	–	–	–	–
ŠAMŠI-ADAD														
Temple of Dagan	–	–	–	–	–	–	–	–	–	–	–	–	–	–
Šubat-Šamaš	–	–	–	–	–	–	–	–	–	–	–	–	–	–
Šubat-Šamaš II	–	–	–	–	–	–	–	–	–	–	–	–	–	–
Mari	–	–	–	–	–	–	–	–	–	–	–	–	–	–
Unknown year	–	–	–	–	–	–	–	–	–	–	–	–	–	–
Unknown year & day	–	–	–	–	–	–	–	–	–	–	–	–	–	–
Unknown day	–	–	–	–	–	–	–	–	–	–	–	–	–	–

	I URĀḪUM	II MALKĀNUM	III LAḪḪUM	IV ABUM	V ḪIBIRTUM	VI IGI.KUR	VII KINŪNUM	VIII DAGAN	IX LILIATUM	X BĒLET-BĪRI	XI KISKISSUM	XII EBĒRUM
YASMAḪ-ADAD (A)												
Ašur-Malik (1)	30	–	15	–	–	–	–	1,30	–	9,15	1,4 5,7+	–
Awīliya (2)	–	–	–	–	–	–	21	–	–	–	–	–
Addu-bani/Census (3)	–	26	–	–	–	–	6	–	20	–	–	–
Asqudum (4)	2,21 30	5,15	15	–	28	–	–	–	1	–	23,25	1,11 30
Ennam-Ašur (5)	–	–	–	–	–	–	–	–	–	–	–	–
Ḫali-Malik (6)	–	–	–	–	–	–	–	–	–	–	–	–
Ikupiya (7)	–	–	–	–	–	–	–	–	–	5,14 15	–	–
Ikūn-pī-Sin (8)	–	–	–	–	–	–	–	–	–	–	–	–
Ili-ellati (9)	–	–	–	–	–	–	–	–	–	–	–	–
Ibni-Addu (10)	–	–	–	–	–	–	–	–	–	–	–	–
Murikmānu/Rikmānu (11)	–	–	–	–	–	–	–	–	–	–	–	–
Nimar-Sin/Nimer-Sin (12)	–	–	–	–	–	–	–	–	–	–	–	–
Puṣṣanum (13)	–	–	–	–	–	–	24	–	–	–	–	–
Šalim-Ašar A (14)	–	–	–	–	–	–	–	–	–	–	–	–
Šalim-Aśar B (15)	–	–	–	–	–	–	–	–	–	–	–	–
Ṭāb-ṣilli-Ašur (16)	–	–	–	5	9,10 11,16+	8,11	15	–	–	–	–	17
Ṭab-ṣilli-Ašur II (17)	–	–	–	–	–	13,14 17,18+	1,4 7+	5,9 11,14+	3,4 5,7+	–	–	–
Nergal (date-year)	–	–	–	–	–	–	–	–	–	–	–	–
Aḫi-Aya	–	–	–	–	–	–	–	–	–	–	–	–
Unknown limu/year	–	–	–	6,8 16,30	–	–	3,10 12,14+	4,23	–	–	16	–
Unknown limu/year & day	–	–	–	1,2 3	–	–	1,2 3,30	1	–	–	–	–
Unknown day	–	–	–	+	–	–	–	–	–	–	–	–

YASMAḪ-ADAD (B)

	I MANA	II AYĀRUM	III MAQRĀNUM	IV DUMUZI		VI TĪRUM		VIII MAMMĪTUM	IX NIQMUM	X TAMḪĪRUM	XI NABRÛ	XII ADDARU	(DIRIG.GA) Intercalary	P/BIRIZARRU (TERQA)
Ašur-Malik (1)	21	24	17	–	–	–	–	–	–	–	–	–	–	–
Awīliya (2)	5,14 15,18+	3	–	–	–	–	–	–	–	–	–	14	–	–
Addu-bani/ Census (3)	1,10 30	5,6	4,5 6,7+	–	–	–	–	1,10	–	10	1	1,23	–	–
Asqudum (4)	–	–	–	–	–	–	–	–	–	–	–	–	–	–
Ennam-Ašur (5)	–	–	–	–	–	–	–	–	–	–	–	–	–	–
Ḫali-Malik (6)	–	–	–	–	–	–	–	–	–	–	–	–	–	–
Ikupiya (7)	–	–	–	–	–	–	–	–	–	–	1	–	–	–
Ikūn-pī-Sin (8)	–	–	–	–	–	–	–	–	–	–	–	–	–	–
Ili-ellati (9)	–	–	–	–	–	–	–	3	–	–	–	–	–	–
Ibni-Addu (10)	–	–	–	–	–	–	–	–	–	–	–	–	–	–
Murikmānu/ Rikmānu (11)	–	–	–	–	–	–	–	–	–	–	–	–	–	–
Nimar-Sin/ Nimer-Sin (12)	27	–	12	–	–	23	–	–	–	–	–	–	–	–
Puṣṣanum (13)	–	–	–	–	–	–	–	–	–	–	–	–	–	–
Šalim-Ašur A (14)	–	–	–	–	–	–	–	–	–	–	–	–	–	–
Šalim-Ašur B (15)	–	–	–	–	–	–	–	–	–	–	–	–	–	–
Ṭāb-ṣilli-Ašur (16)	–	–	–	–	–	–	–	–	–	–	–	–	–	–
Ṭāb-ṣilli-Ašur II (17)	–	–	–	–	–	–	–	1,6 7	–	11	–	–	–	–
Nergal (date year)	–	–	–	–	–	–	–	–	–	–	–	–	–	20
Aḫi-Aya	–	24	–	3	–	–	–	1	–	22	–	–	–	–
Unknown limu/ year	5,18 22,25	4,5 8,24+	4	2,4 5,8,30+	–	15,20	–	3,20 22,25	25,26	20,21	–	3,12 16,20+	19	–
Unknown limu/ year and day	1	–	1,2	–	–	–	–	1,2	–	–	–	–	–	–
Unknown day	+	+	+	+	–	+	–	+	+	+	+	+	–	–

ZIMRI-LIM

	I URĀḪUM	II MALKĀNUM	III LAḪḪUM	IV ABUM	V ḪIBIRTUM	VI IGI.KUR	VII KINŪNUM	VIII DAGAN	IX LILIATUM	X BĒLET-BĪRI	XI KISKISSUM	XII EBŪRUM	V ḪIBIRTUM II (Intercalary)	XII EBŪRUM II (Intercalary)	P/BIRIZARRU (TERQA)	ADNATUM
Euphrates (29)	—	—	—	15,20	—	—	—	—	—	11,24	23,28 29,30+	2,4	—	—	—	—
Benjaminites (6)	4,5 6,8+	1,2 3,7+	7,8 10,11+	13	6	—	6	8,21 27,28+	1,3 4,5+	1,2 3,4+	2,3 5,6+	1,2 3,5+	—	20,21 23,24	—	—
Benjaminites II (7)	12	—	—	—	16	25	—	20,30	—	—	—	—	—	—	—	—
Ašlakka (2)	4,20 21.27	2,5	—	—	—	—	—	30	17,28	5,9 10,15+	8,14 27	5,20 21	—	—	—	10
Aslakka II (3)	19	26		—	—	—	—	—	—	—	—	—	—	—	—	
Throne of Šamaš (16)	10,11 20,26+		1,2 3,4+	1,4 5,9+	1,2+	3,4	4,8 10,12+	1,5 12,13	1,3 4,5+	1,2 4,5	1,5 6,8+	1,2+	—	—	—	—
Throne of Šamaš II (17)	—	3	—	—	—		—	—	—	—	—	—	—	—	—	—
Census (26)	1,2 3,4+	1+	1,5 9,11+	1,4 6,7	1,2+	1,10 12,16	1,14 18,20+	1,6 8,10+	1,2 4,7+	1,3 6,9+	1,2+	1,2	—	—	—	—
Dūr-Yaḫdun-Lim (28)	1,3 4,5+	1,2 4,5+	6,9 10,11+	1,2 5,6+	1,2 4,6+	1+	1,2 7,8+	1,9 15,19+	1,3 4,5+	2,3 4,5+	1,2 3,4+	1+	—	—	—	—
Ḫatta (21)	1,2 6,8+	1+	4,5 8,9+	3,4 6,7+	2,3 4,5+	4,7 10,14+	2,26 29,30	6,8 10,16	1,2+	6,8 9,10+	1,2 3,4+	1+	—	—	—	—
Ḫatta II (21b)	3	—	—	—	—		—	—	—	—	—	—	—	—	—	—
Elam Expedition (13)	1,9 11,20+	6,16 26	7,8 9,10+	2,4 18,19+	2,4 6,7+	2,3 7,8+	24	26	15	13	—	—	—	—	—	—
Addu of Maḫanum (18)	24	10	—	—	—	—	5	2,15	29	20	—	7,24 30	—	—	—	—
Babylon (11)	4,10	16	—	8,10	—	—	8,28 30	28	20,24	25	—	13	6,24	—	—	—
Babylon II (12)	—	—	23,29	—	—	—	—	—	—	—	—	—	—	—	—	—
Throne of Dagan (14)	9,22	10	—	—	5,29	4,6 7,12+	2	—	25	—	29	23	17	—	—	—
Throne of Dagan II (15)	7	—	—	—	—	—	—	—	—	—	—	—	—	—	—	—
IInd Aślakka (3b)	29	—	—	1	5,6	—	—	—	—	—	—	—	—	—	—	—
Throne of his father (1)	—	—	—	—	—	—	—	30	—	—	—	—	—	—	—	—
Kaḫat (4)	—	—	—	—	—	—	—	—	—	27	3,8 11,12	3	—	—	—	—
Kaḫat II (4b)	18,24	—	—	—	—	—	—	—	—	—	—	—	—	—	—	—
Mišlān (5)	—	21	—	—	—	—	—	—	—	—	—	—	—	—	—	—
Elam Victory (8)	—	—	—	—	—	—	—	—	—	—	—	—	—	—	—	—
Elaḫut Victory (9)	—	—	—	—	—	—	—	29	—	—	17,18	—	—	—	2	—
Qarni-Lim (10)	—	—	—	—	—	—	—	—	—	—	—	—	—	—	—	—
IInd Babylon (12b)	—	—	—	1,3 24	—	—	—	—	—	—	—	—	—	—	—	—
Throne of Diritum (19)	—	—	—	—	—	—	—	—	—	—	—	—	—	—	—	—
Addu of Ḫalab (20)	—	—	—	—	9	—	13	10	—	—	—	—	—	—	—	—
Annunitum of Šeḫrum (22)	—	10	22	—	—	—	—	22	—	—	—	—	—	—	—	—
Addu of Appan (23)	—	—	—	—	—	—	—	—	—	—	—	—	—	—	—	—
Addu of Appan II (24)	—	—	—	—	1	—	—	—	—	—	—	—	—	—	—	—
Lions of Dagan (25)	—	—	—	—	—	—	—	—	—	—	—	—	—	—	—	—
Saramā (27)	—	—	—	—	—	—	—	—	—	—	—	—	—	—	—	—
Ḫabur (30)	—	—	—	1	—	1	—	—	—	—	—	—	—	—	—	—
Muballittum (31)	1+	1+	—	—	—	—	—	—	15	—	—	—	—	—	—	—
Yamḫad (32)	—	—	—	22	1	—	—	—	—	—	—	—	—	—	—	—
Andariq (33)	—	—	—	—	—	—	—	—	—	—	—	—	—	—	—	—
Census II (26b)	9	—	—	—	—	—	—	—	—	—	—	—	—	—	—	—
Unknown year	1,8+	1+	1,4 5,6+	1,2 4,5+	1,2 3,5+	1,5 6,9+	2,3 4,7+	1,3 4,6+	2,3 9,10+	2,5 12,13+	2,3 4,5+	1+	8	21	27	—
Unknown year and day	1,2 3,5+	2,6 7,8+	1,2 3,4+	1,2 3,4+	1,2 3,4+	1,2 3,4	1,2 3,4+	1,2 3,4+	1,2 3,4+	1,2 3,4+	1,2 3,4+	1,2 3,4+	—	—	1	—
Unknown day	+	+	+	+	+	+	+	+	+	+	+	+	—	+	—	—

To reduce costs, months for which no dated texts are known at present do not have a corresponding sheet in this book. They are, however, taken into consideration as far as the pagination of the book is concerned, as shown in the following table. They are also included in the "Summary Tabulation of Dates by Years and Months" given above as Appendix B.

In order to allow the user to update the volume entries in the measure in which new dated texts are published, the reverse of this page may be duplicated and used as needed. The "blank" months are as follows:

King	Month	Page
Yaḫdun-Lim	I URĀḪUM	1*
Yaḫdun-Lim	II MALKĀNUM	2*
Yaḫdun-Lim	V ḪIBIRTUM	5*
Yaḫdun-Lim	VI IGI.KUR	6*
Yaḫdun-Lim	VII KINŪNUM	7*
Yaḫdun-Lim	IX LILIATUM	9*
Yaḫdun-Lim	X BĒLET-BĪRI	10*
Yaḫdun-Lim	XII EBŪRUM	12*
Yaḫdun-Lim	–	13*
Yaḫdun-Lim	–	14*
Sumu-Yamam/Šamši-Adad	III LAḪḪUM	17*
Sumu-Yamam/Šamši-Adad	IV ABUM	18*
Sumu-Yamam/Šamši-Adad	VII KINŪNUM	21*
Sumu-Yamam/Šašmi-Adad	XI KISKISSUM	25*
Sumu-Yamam/Šamši-Adad	XII EBŪRUM	26*
Sumu-Yamam/Šamši-Adad	–	29*
Sumu-Yamam/Šamši-Adad	–	30*
Yasmaḫ-Adad	I URĀḪUM (2)	32*
Yasmaḫ-Adad	II MALKĀNUM (2)	34*
Yasmaḫ-Adad	III LAḪḪUM (2)	36*
Yasmaḫ-Adad	V ḪIBIRTUM (2)	40*
Yasmaḫ-Adad	VI IGI.KUR (2)	42*
Yasmaḫ-Adad	IX LILIATUM (2)	48*
Yasmaḫ-Adad	X BĒLET-BĪRI (2)	50*
Yasmaḫ-Adad	XII EBŪRUM	54*
Yasmaḫ-Adad	–	55*
Yasmaḫ-Adad	–	56*
Yasmaḫ-Adad	IV DUMUZI (1)	63*
Yasmaḫ-Adad	IX NIQMUM (1)	69*
Yasmaḫ-Adad	(DIRIG.GA) (1) Intercalary	77*
Yasmaḫ-Adad	P/BIRIZARRU (TERQA) (2)	80*
Zimri-Lim[1]	V ḪIBIRTUM II Intercalary (2)	118*
Zimri-Lim[1]	XII EBŪRUM II Intercalary (2)	121*
Zimri-Lim	P/BIRIZARRU (TERQA) (1)	123*
Zimri-Lim	ADNATUM (2)	127*
Zimri-Lim	ADNATUM (3)	128*
Zimri-Lim	–	129*
Zimri-Lim	–	130*
Zimri-Lim	–	131*

[1] These two months are reproduced in the body of the text, even though they are blank, in order to have a complete set of the main months of Zimri-Lim.

III LAḪḪUM

	1	2	3	4	5	6	7	8	9	10	11	12	13	14	15	16	17	18	19	20	21	22	23	24	25	26	27	28	29	30
Yaḫdun-Lim																														
Paḫudar (#1)																														
Zalma[ ] (#2)																														
Zalpaḫ (#3)																														
Imar (#4)																														
Zab[ ] (#5)																														
Ḫen/Benjaminites (#6)															[VIII:51]a LL															
Šamši-Addu (#7)																														
Šamaš																														
Šamaš II																														
Benjaminites																														
Nagar																														
Unknown year																				[VIII:48] LL										
Unknown year and day																														
Unknown day																														
Išar-Lim																														
Kingship																														

	1	2	3	4	5	6	7	8	9	10	11	12	13	14	15	16	17	18	19	20	21	22	23	24	25	26	27	28	29	30
Yaḫdun-Lim																														
Paḫudar (#1)																														
Zalma[ ] (#2)																														
Zalpaḫ (#3)				VII:1 R																										
Imar (#4)																														
Zab[ ] (#5)																														
Ḫen/Benjaminites (#6)																														
Šamši-Addu (#7)																														
Šamaš																														
Šamaš II															VIII:61c LL															
Benjaminites																														
Nagar																														
Unknown year																														
Unknown year and day																														
Unknown day																														
Išar-Lim																														
Kingship																														

	1	2	3	4	5	6	7	8	9	10	11	12	13	14	15	16	17	18	19	20	21	22	23	24	25	26	27	28	29	30
Yaḫdun-Lim																														
Paḫudar (#1)																														
Zalma[ ] (#2)																														
Zalpaḫ (#3)																														
Imar (#4)																														
Zab[ ] (#5)																														
Ḫen/Benjaminites (#6)																														
Šamši-Addu (#7)																														
Šamaš																														
Šamaš II																														
Benjaminites																														
Nagar																														
Unknown year																														
Unknown year and day																														
Unknown day	VIII:55 ZALPAḪ LL																													
Išar-Lim																														
Kingship																														

	1	2	3	4	5	6	7	8	9	10	11	12	13	14	15	16	17	18	19	20	21	22	23	24	25	26	27	28	29	30
Yaḫdun-Lim																														
Paḫudar (#1)																														
Zalma[ ] (#2)																														
Zalpaḫ (#3)																													VIII:70 L	
Imar (#4)																														
Zab[ ] (#5)																														
Ḫen/Benjaminites (#6)																														
Šamši-Addu (#7)																														
Šamaš																														
Šamaš II																														
Benjaminites																														
Nagar																														
Unknown year																														
Unknown year and day																														
Unknown day	VIII:75 BENJ A/L																													
Išar-Lim																														
Kingship																														

Sumu-Yamam

	1	2	3	4	5	6	7	8	9	10	11	12	13	14	15	16	17	18	19	20	21	22	23	24	25	26	27	28	29	30
Ḫalabit									RA 65 p. 55 A/p										RA 65 p. 55 A/p										RA 65 p. 55 A/p	
Saggaratum																														
Saggaratum II																														
Unknown year																														
Unknown year and day																														
Unknown day																														
Šamši-Adad																														
Temple of Dagan																														
Šubat-Šamaš																														
Šubat-Šamaš II																														
Mari																														
Unknown year																														
Unknown year and day																														
Unknown day																														

Sumu-Yamam

	1	2	3	4	5	6	7	8	9	10	11	12	13	14	15	16	17	18	19	20	21	22	23	24	25	26	27	28	29	30
Ḫalabit																														
Saggaratum																														
Saggaratum II																														
Unknown year																														
Unknown year and day	[cf. Kupper de Liagre Böhl, 267 n. 6]																													
Unknown day																														
Šamši-Adad																														
Temple of Dagan																														
Šubat-Šamaš																														
Šubat-Šamaš II																														
Mari																														
Unknown year																														
Unknown year and day																														
Unknown day																														

V ḪIBIRTUM

Sumu-Yamam

	1	2	3	4	5	6	7	8	9	10	11	12	13	14	15	16	17	18	19	20	21	22	23	24	25	26	27	28	29	30
Ḫalabit																														
Saggaratum																														
Saggaratum II																														
Unknown year																														
Unknown year and day	[cf. KUPPER in LIAGRE BÖHL, p.267 n.4]																													
Unknown day																														

Šamši-Adad

	1	2	3	4	5	6	7	8	9	10	11	12	13	14	15	16	17	18	19	20	21	22	23	24	25	26	27	28	29	30
Temple of Dagan																														
Šubat-Šamaš																														
Šubat-Šamaš II																														
Mari																														
Unknown year																														
Unknown year and day																														
Unknown day																														

Sumu-Yamam

	1	2	3	4	5	6	7	8	9	10	11	12	13	14	15	16	17	18	19	20	21	22	23	24	25	26	27	28	29	30
Ḫalabit									RA 64,34 A																					
Saggaratum																														
Saggaratum II																														
Unknown year																														
Unknown year and day																														
Unknown day																														
Šamši-Adad																														
Temple of Dagan																														
Šubat-Šamaš																														
Šubat-Šamaš II																														
Mari																														
Unknown year																														
Unknown year and day																														
Unknown day																														

Sumu-Yamam

	1	2	3	4	5	6	7	8	9	10	11	12	13	14	15	16	17	18	19	20	21	22	23	24	25	26	27	28	29	30
Ḫalabit			RA 64, 4 A																											
Saggaratum															RA 65 p. 64 A/r															
Saggaratum II																														
Unknown year																														
Unknown year and day																														
Unknown day																														
Šamši-Adad																														
Temple of Dagan																														
Šubat-Šamaš																														
Šubat-Šamaš II																														
Mari																														
Unknown year																														
Unknown year and day																														
Unknown day																														

IX LILIATUM

Sumu-Yamam

	1	2	3	4	5	6	7	8	9	10	11	12	13	14	15	16	17	18	19	20	21	22	23	24	25	26	27	28	29	30
Ḫalabit																														
Saggaratum									RA 64,29 A/o																					
Saggaratum II																														
Unknown year															RA 64,33 A/o															
Unknown year and day																														
Unknown day																														
Šamši-Adad																														
Temple of Dagan																														
Šubat-Šamaš																														
Šubat-Šamaš II																														
Mari																														
Unknown year																														
Unknown year and day																														
Unknown day																														

Sumu-Yamam

	1	2	3	4	5	6	7	8	9	10	11	12	13	14	15	16	17	18	19	20	21	22	23	24	25	26	27	28	29	30
Halabit					RA 64,9 A																									
Saggaratum																														
Saggaratum II																														
Unknown year																														
Unknown year and day																														
Unknown day																														
Šamši-Adad																														
Temple of Dagan																														
Šubat-Šamaš																														
Šubat-Šamaš II																														
Mari																														
Unknown year																														
Unknown year and day																														
Unknown day																														

Sumu-Yamam

	1	2	3	4	5	6	7	8	9	10	11	12	13	14	15	16	17	18	19	20	21	22	23	24	25	26	27	28	29	30
Ḫalabit															RA 64,11 A														RA 64,17 A	
Saggaratum																														
Saggaratum II																														
Unknown year																														
Unknown year and day																														
Unknown day																														
Šamši-Adad																														
Temple of Dagan																														
Šubat-Šamaš																														
Šubat-Šamaš II																														
Mari																														
Unknown year																														
Unknown year and day																														
Unknown day																														

EBŪRUM II (Intercalary)

Sumu-Yamam

	1	2	3	4	5	6	7	8	9	10	11	12	13	14	15	16	17	18	19	20	21	22	23	24	25	26	27	28	29	30
Ḫalabit																														
Saggaratum								RA 64,18 A ↓							RA 64,21 A ↓															
Saggaratum II	RA 64,28 ,1 ,6 Rk A A	RA 64,7 ,25 A A		RA 64,32 A/o	RA 64,26 ,8 R/o A	RA 64,20 A		RA 64,12 ,14 ,15 A A A	RA 64,24 A			RA 64,22 A	RA 64,5 A?	RA 64,10 ,19 A A	RA 64,27 ,31 ,2 R/o A A/o															
Unknown year																														
Unknown year and day	RA 64,30 R?																													
Unknown day	RA 64,16 SAG II A	RA 64,23 SAG II A																												
Šamši-Adad																														
Temple of Dagan																														
Šubat-Šamaš																														
Šubat-Šamaš II																														
Mari																														
Unknown year																														
Unknown year and day																														
Unknown day																														

I URĀḪUM (1)

Yasmaḫ-Adad	1	2	3	4	5	6	7	8	9	10	11	12	13	14	15	16	17	18	19	20	21	22	23	24	25	26	27	28	29	30
Ašur-Malik (#1)																														XI:5 F/R
Awīliya (#2)																														
Addu-bani/ Census (#3)																														
Asqudum (#4)		XII:9 Fc/R																			XII:10 F/P									XII:11 Fc/P
Ennam-Ašur (#5)																														
Ḫali-Malik (#6)																														
Ikupiya (#7)																														
Ikūn-pī-Sin (#8)																														
Ili-ellati (#9)																														
Ibni-Addu (#10)																														
Murikmānu/Rikmānu (#11)																														
Nimar-Sin/ Nimer-Sin (#12)																														
Puṣṣanum (#13)																														
Šalim-Ašar A (#14)																														
Šalim-Ašar B (#15)																														
Ṭāb-ṣilli-Ašur (#16)																														
Ṭāb-ṣilli-Ašur II (#17)																														
Nergal (date-year)																														

II MALKĀNUM (1)

Yasmaḫ-Adad	1	2	3	4	5	6	7	8	9	10	11	12	13	14	15	16	17	18	19	20	21	22	23	24	25	26	27	28	29	30
Ašur-Malik (#1)																														
Awīliya (#2)																														
Addu-bani/ Census (#3)																										VII:7 Fo/t				
Asqudum (#4)					XII:12 Fc/P										XI:11 F/P															
Ennam-Ašur (#5)																														
Ḫali-Malik (#6)																														
Ikupiya (#7)																														
Ikūn-pī-Sin (#8)																														
Ili-ellati (#9)																														
Ibni-Addu (#10)																														
Murikmānu/Rikmānu (#11)																														
Nimar-Sin/ Nimer-Sin (#12)																														
Puṣṣanum (#13)																														
Šalim-Ašar A (#14)																														
Šalim-Ašar B (#15)																														
Ṭāb-ṣilli-Ašur (#16)																														
Ṭāb-ṣilli-Ašur II (#17)																														
Nergal (date-year)																														

Yasmaḫ-Adad	1	2	3	4	5	6	7	8	9	10	11	12	13	14	15	16	17	18	19	20	21	22	23	24	25	26	27	28	29	30
Ašur-Malik (#1)															[VII:2] Ao/P															
Awīliya (#2)																														
Addu-bani/ Census (#3)																														
Asqudum (#4)															XII:13 Fc/R															
Ennam-Ašur (#5)																														
Ḫali-Malik (#6)																														
Ikupiya (#7)																														
Ikūn-pī-Sin (#8)																														
Ili-ellati (#9)																														
Ibni-Addu (#10)																														
Murikmānu/Rikmānu (#11)																														
Nimar-Sin/ Nimer-Sin (#12)																														
Puṣṣanum (#13)																														
Šalim-Ašar A (#14)																														
Šalim-Ašar B (#15)																														
Ṭāb-ṣilli-Ašur (#16)																														
Ṭāb-ṣilli-Ašur II (#17)																														
Nergal (date-year)																														

Yasmaḫ-Adad	1	2	3	4	5	6	7	8	9	10	11	12	13	14	15	16	17	18	19	20	21	22	23	24	25	26	27	28	29	30
Ašur-Malik (#1)																														
Awīliya (#2)																														
Addu-bani/ Census (#3)																														
Asqudum (#4)																														
Ennam-Ašur (#5)																														
Ḫali-Malik (#6)																														
Ikupiya (#7)																														
Ikūn-pī-Sin (#8)																														
Ili-ellati (#9)																														
Ibni-Addu (#10)																														
Murikmānu/Rikmānu (#11)																														
Nimar-Sin/ Nimer-Sin (#12)																														
Puṣṣanum (#13)																														
Šalim-Ašar A (#14)																														
Šalim-Ašar B (#15)																														
Ṭāb-ṣilli-Ašur (#16)					VII:12 Ȧo/P													VII:13 Ao/P												
Ṭāb-ṣilli-Ašur II (#17)																														
Nergal (date-year)																														

Yasmaḫ-Adad	1	2	3	4	5	6	7	8	9	10	11	12	13	14	15	16	17	18	19	20	21	22	23	24	25	26	27	28	29	30
Aḫi-Aya																														
Unknown limu/year						I:67 E		I:5 E								I:19 E														II:8 E
Unknown limu/year +day	[VIII:39] LL	XIII:139 Lt	[VIII:34] Lℓ																											
Unknown day	CBA 923 A·BANI A	CBA 963 A-BANI Ac	CBA 966 A-BANI Ac	CBA 968 A-BANI Ac																										

V ḪIBIRTUM (1)

Yasmaḫ-Adad	1	2	3	4	5	6	7	8	9	10	11	12	13	14	15	16	17	18	19	20	21	22	23	24	25	26	27	28	29	30
Ašur-Malik (#1)																														
Awīliya (#2)																														
Addu-bani/ Census (#3)																														
Asqudum (#4)																												VIII:1 L		
Ennam-Ašur (#5)																														
Ḫali-Malik (#6)																														
Ikupiya (#7)																														
Ikūn-pī-Sin (#8)																														
Ili-ellati (#9)																														
Ibni-Addu (#10)																														
Murikmānu/Rikmānu (#11)																														
Nimar-Sin/ Nimer-Sin (#12)																														
Puṣṣanum (#13)																														
Šalim-Ašar A (#14)																														
Šalim-Ašar B (#15)																														
Ṭāb-ṣilli-Ašur (#16)									VII:14 Ao/p	VII:15 Ao/R	VII:16 Ao/R					VII:17 Ao/p				VII:18 Ao/pš		VII:19 Ao/p					VII:20 Ao/š	VII:21 Ao/p		
Ṭāb-ṣilli-Ašur II (#17)																														
Nergal (date-year)																														

Yasmaḫ-Adad	1	2	3	4	5	6	7	8	9	10	11	12	13	14	15	16	17	18	19	20	21	22	23	24	25	26	27	28	29	30
Ašur-Malik (#1)																														
Awīliya (#2)																														
Addu-bani/ Census (#3)																														
Asqudum (#4)																														
Ennam-Ašur (#5)																														
Ḫali-Malik (#6)																														
Ikupiya (#7)																														
Ikūn-pī-Sin (#8)																														
Ili-ellati (#9)																														
Ibni-Addu (#10)																														
Murikmānu/Rikmānu (#11)																														
Nimar-Sin/ Nimer-Sin (#12)																														
Puṣṣanum (#13)																														
Šalim-Ašar A (#14)																														
Šalim-Ašar B (#15)																														
Ṭāb-ṣilli-Ašur (#16)								VII:22 Ao/p		VII:23 Ao/p																				
Ṭāb-ṣilli-Ašur II (#17)													VII:40 Ao/p	VII:41 Ao/š		VII:42 Ao/p	VII:43 Ao/R		VII:44 Ao/R		VII:45 Ao/š,p		VII:46 Ao/š	VII:47 Ao/š				VII:48 Ao/p		
Nergal (date-year)																														

Yasmaḫ-Adad	1	2	3	4	5	6	7	8	9	10	11	12	13	14	15	16	17	18	19	20	21	22	23	24	25	26	27	28	29	30
Ašur-Malik (#1)																														
Awīliya (#2)																					VIII:9 Lp									
Addu-bani/ Census (#3)						VII:8 Ao/š,R																								
Asqudum (#4)																														
Ennam-Ašur (#5)																														
Ḫali-Malik (#6)																														
Ikupiya (#7)																														
Ikūn-pī-Sin (#8)																														
Ili-ellati (#9)																														
Ibni-Addu (#10)																														
Murikmānu/Rikmānu (#11)																														
Nimar-Sin/ Nimer-Sin (#12)																														
Puṣṣanum (#13)																								VIII:86 L						
Šalim-Ašar A (#14)																														
Šalim-Ašar B (#15)																														
Ṭāb-ṣilli-Ašur (#16)															VII:24 Ao/p															
Ṭāb-ṣilli-Ašur II (#17)	VII:62 :63 Ao/š Ab/p		VII:64 Ao/R,š	VII:65 Ao/š				VII:66 Ao/R	VII:67 Ao/p			VII:68 :69 Ao/p Ao		VII:70 Ao/R	VII:71 :72 Ao/R Ao/R			VII:73 :74 Ao/R Ao/p		VII:75 Ao/p	VII:76 :77 Ao/p Ao/R									
Nergal (date-year)																														

Yasmaḫ-Adad	1	2	3	4	5	6	7	8	9	10	11	12	13	14	15	16	17	18	19	20	21	22	23	24	25	26	27	28	29	30
Aḫi-Aya																														
Unknown limu/year			I:53 E							IV:35 E		V:83 E		SYRIA 50 p 278 E						IV:18 E										
Unknown limu/year +day	[II:6] E	IV:19 E	CBA 985 Ac																											[II:6] E
Unknown day																														

VIII DAGAN (1)

Yasmaḫ-Adad	1	2	3	4	5	6	7	8	9	10	11	12	13	14	15	16	17	18	19	20	21	22	23	24	25	26	27	28	29	30
Ašur-Malik (#1)		XI:6 Fe/R																												XII:6 F/A
Awīliya (#2)																														
Addu-bani/ Census (#3)																														
Asqudum (#4)																														
Ennam-Ašur (#5)																														
Ḫali-Malik (#6)																														
Ikupiya (#7)																														
Ikūn-pī-Sin (#8)																														
Ili-ellati (#9)																														
Ibni-Addu (#10)																														
Murikmānu/Rikmānu (#11)																														
Nimar-Sin/ Nimer-Sin (#12)																														
Puṣṣanum (#13)																														
Šalim-Ašar A (#14)																														
Šalim-Ašar B (#15)																														
Ṭāb-ṣilli-Ašur (#16)																														
Ṭāb-ṣilli-Ašur II (#17)					VII:49 Ao/p				VII:50 :51 Ao/R Ao/p		VII:52 Ao/R			VII:53 :54 Ao/p Ao/p						VII:55 Ao/p(R?)	VII:56 Ao/p			[VII:57] Ao/p	VII:58 Ao/R		VII:59 Ao/š			VII:60 :61 Ao/R Ao/p
Nergal (date-year)																														

VIII <u>DAGAN</u> (2)

Yasmaḫ-Adad	1	2	3	4	5	6	7	8	9	10	11	12	13	14	15	16	17	18	19	20	21	22	23	24	25	26	27	28	29	30
Aḫi-Aya																														
Unknown limu/year				VII:85 Ao																			VII:84 Ao/p							
Unknown limu/year +day	I:34 E																													
Unknown day																														

IX LILIATUM (1)

Yasmaḫ-Adad	1	2	3	4	5	6	7	8	9	10	11	12	13	14	15	16	17	18	19	20	21	22	23	24	25	26	27	28	29	30
Ašur-Malik (#1)																														
Awīliya (#2)																														
Addu-bani/ Census (#3)																				VII:6 Ao/R										
Asqudum (#4)	VII:9 Rk																													
Ennam-Ašur (#5)																														
Ḫali-Malik (#6)																														
Ikupiya (#7)																														
Ikūn-pī-Sin (#8)																														
Ili-ellati (#9)																														
Ibni-Addu (#10)																														
Murikmānu/Rikmānu (#11)																														
Nimar-Sin/ Nimer-Sin (#12)																														
Puṣṣanum (#13)																														
Šalim-Ašar A (#14)																														
Šalim-Ašar B (#15)																														
Ṭāb-ṣilli-Ašur (#16)																														
Ṭāb-ṣilli-Ašur II (#17)			[VII:39] Ao	VII:25 :26 Ao/Š Ao	VII:27 :28 Ao/P Ao/R		VII:29 :30 Ao/R Ao/P				VII:31 Ao/P		[VII:39] Ao				VII:32 :33 Ao/P Ao/P			VII:34 Ao/P	VII:35 :36 Ao/P Ao/R		[VII:39] Ao	VII:37 Ao/P	VII:38 Ao/P					
Nergal (date-year)																														

X BĒLET-BĪRI (1)

Yasmaḫ-Adad	1	2	3	4	5	6	7	8	9	10	11	12	13	14	15	16	17	18	19	20	21	22	23	24	25	26	27	28	29	30
Ašur-Malik (#1)									XII:1 Fms						XII:2 Fms															
Awīliya (#2)																														
Addu-bani/ Census (#3)																														
Asqudum (#4)																														
Ennam-Ašur (#5)																														
Ḫali-Malik (#6)																														
Ikupiya (#7)					[XII:14] Fms										[XII:14] Fms										[XII:14] Fms					
Ikūn-pī-Sin (#8)																														
Ili-ellati (#9)																														
Ibni-Addu (#10)																														
Murikmānu/Rikmānu (#11)																														
Nimar-Sin/ Nimer-Sin (#12)																														
Puṣṣanum (#13)																														
Šalim-Ašar A (#14)																														
Šalim-Ašar B (#15)																														
Ṭāb-ṣilli-Ašur (#16)																														
Ṭāb-ṣilli-Ašur II (#17)																														
Nergal (date-year)																														

XI KISKISSUM (1)

Yasmaḫ-Adad	1	2	3	4	5	6	7	8	9	10	11	12	13	14	15	16	17	18	19	20	21	22	23	24	25	26	27	28	29	30
Ašur-Malik (#1)	XII:3 F/R/c			XI:1 :2 Fms F/R	XII:4 Fms		XI:3 Fms	XI:4 Fms						[XII:5] F/p											[XII:7] Fs/t		[XII:7] Fs/t			
Awīliya (#2)																														
Addu-bani/ Census (#3)																														
Asqudum (#4)																							XI:7 Fms		XI:8 Fm/t					
Ennam-Ašur (#5)																														
Ḫali-Malik (#6)																														
Ikupiya (#7)																														
Ikūn-pī-Sin (#8)																														
Ili-ellati (#9)																														
Ibni-Addu (#10)																														
Murikmānu/Rikmānu (#11)																														
Nimar-Sin/ Nimer-Sin (#12)																														
Puṣṣanum (#13)																														
Šalim-Ašar A (#14)																														
Šalim-Ašar B (#15)																														
Ṭāb-ṣilli-Ašur (#16)																														
Ṭāb-ṣilli-Ašur II (#17)																														
Nergal (date-year)																														

XI KISKISSUM (2)

Yasmaḫ-Adad	1	2	3	4	5	6	7	8	9	10	11	12	13	14	15	16	17	18	19	20	21	22	23	24	25	26	27	28	29	30
Aḫi-Aya																														
Unknown limu/year																[VIII:34] LL														
Unknown limu/year +day																														
Unknown day																														

XII EBŪRUM (1)

Yasmaḫ-Adad	1	2	3	4	5	6	7	8	9	10	11	12	13	14	15	16	17	18	19	20	21	22	23	24	25	26	27	28	29	30
Ašur-Malik (#1)																														
Awīliya (#2)																														
Addu-bani/ Census (#3)																														
Asqudum (#4)	XI:9 Fc										XII:8 Fms																			XI:10 F/R?
Ennam-Ašur (#5)																														
Ḫali-Malik (#6)																														
Ikupiya (#7)																														
Ikūn-pī-Sin (#8)																														
Ili-ellati (#9)																														
Ibni-Addu (#10)																														
Murikmānu/Rikmānu (#11)																														
Nimar-Sin/ Nimer-Sin (#12)																														
Puṣṣanum (#13)																														
Šalim-Ašar A (#14)																														
Šalim-Ašar B (#15)																														
Ṭāb-ṣilli-Ašur (#16)																	VII:11 Ao/R													
Ṭāb-ṣilli-Ašur II (#17)																														
Nergal (date-year)																														

Yasmaḫ-Adad	1	2	3	4	5	6	7	8	9	10	11	12	13	14	15	16	17	18	19	20	21	22	23	24	25	26	27	28	29	30
Ašur-Malik (#1)																					VII:4 A/R									
Awīliya (#2)					CBA 381! Ac/p									VII:5 Ao/R	CBA 380 Ac/p			[CBA 994 A/c	→	→		[CBA 994] A/c			[CBA 994] A/c					
Addu-bani/ Census (#3)	CBA 920a CBA 934 CBA 964 Ac/p A Ac									CBA 933 A																				CBA 971 F/R
Asqudum (#4)																														
Ennam-Ašur (#5)																														
Ḫali-Malik (#6)																														
Ikupiya (#7)																														
Ikūn-pī-Sin (#8)																														
Ili-ellati (#9)																														
Ibni-Addu (#10)																														
Murikmānu/Rikmānu (#11)																														
Nimar-Sin/ Nimer-Sin (#12)																											CBA 378 Ac/p			
Puṣṣanum (#13)																														
Šalim-Ašar A (#14)																														
Šalim-Ašar B (#15)																														
Ṭāb-ṣilli-Ašur (#16)																														
Ṭāb-ṣilli-Ašur II (#17)																														
Nergal (date-year)																														

Yasmaḫ-Adad	1	2	3	4	5	6	7	8	9	10	11	12	13	14	15	16	17	18	19	20	21	22	23	24	25	26	27	28	29	30
Aḫi-Aya																														
Unknown limu/year					IV:59 E													CBA 994 [Aweliya] Ac				CBA 994 Aweliya Ac			CBA 994 [Aweliya] Ac					
Unknown limu/year +day	1:110 E																													
Unknown day	CBA 955 A-BANI A/R	CBA 974 A-BANI A/p	AOAT 1 p.236:#44 A-BANI A																											

Yasmaḫ-Adad	1	2	3	4	5	6	7	8	9	10	11	12	13	14	15	16	17	18	19	20	21	22	23	24	25	26	27	28	29	30
Ašur-Malik (#1)																								[VIII:50][4] lc						
Awīliya (#2)			[CBA 994] Ac																											
Addu-bani/ Census (#3)					CBA 990 A/R	CBA 926 CBA 978 F5/R A/R																								
Asqudum (#4)																														
Ennam-Ašur (#5)																														
Ḫali-Malik (#6)																														
Ikupiya (#7)																														
Ikūn-pī-Sin (#8)																														
Ili-ellati (#9)																														
Ibni-Addu (#10)																														
Murikmānu/Rikmānu (#11)																														
Nimar-Sin/ Nimer-Sin (#12)																														
Puṣṣanum (#13)																														
Šalim-Ašar A (#14)																														
Šalim-Ašar B (#15)																														
Ṭāb-ṣilli-Ašur (#16)																														
Ṭāb-ṣilli-Ašur II (#17)																														
Nergal (date-year)																														

Yasmaḫ-Adad	1	2	3	4	5	6	7	8	9	10	11	12	13	14	15	16	17	18	19	20	21	22	23	24	25	26	27	28	29	30
Aḫi-Aya																								[VIII:50]? Ll						
Unknown limu/year				1:43 E	1:43 E			1:60 E																VIII:50 LL						1:43? E
Unknown limu/year +day																														
Unknown day	CBA 950 A-BANI F/R	CBA 928 A-BANI A	CBA 996 A-BANI A/R	CBA 920 A-BANI A/P	CBA 949 A-BANI A																									

Yasmaḫ-Adad	1	2	3	4	5	6	7	8	9	10	11	12	13	14	15	16	17	18	19	20	21	22	23	24	25	26	27	28	29	30
Ašur-Malik (#1)																	VII:3 Ao/R													
Awīliya (#2)																														
Addu-bani/ Census (#3)				[CBA 924!] F	[CBA 924] CBA 962 F F	[CBA 921] F	CBA 972 Ac/t		[CBA 921!] F	CBA 945 CBA 953 CBA 981 F A F	CBA 956 935 F F			CBA 927 F	CBA 957 F															
Asqudum (#4)																														
Ennam-Ašur (#5)																														
Ḫali-Malik (#6)																														
Ikupiya (#7)																														
Ikūn-pī-Sin (#8)																														
Ili-ellati (#9)																														
Ibni-Addu (#10)																														
Murikmānu/Rikmānu (#11)																														
Nimar-Sin/ Nimer-Sin (#12)												CBA 932 991 A/P A/P																		
Puṣṣanum (#13)																														
Šalim-Ašar A (#14)																														
Šalim-Ašar B (#15)																														
Ṭāb-ṣilli-Ašur (#16)																														
Ṭāb-ṣilli-Ašur II (#17)																														
Nergal (date-year)																														

Yasmaḫ-Adad	1	2	3	4	5	6	7	8	9	10	11	12	13	14	15	16	17	18	19	20	21	22	23	24	25	26	27	28	29	30
Aḫi-Aya																														
Unknown limu/year				1:39 E																										
Unknown limu/year +day	RA 7, p151-156 E	CBA 925 F																												
Unknown day	CBA 938 A-BANI A	CBA 947 A-BANI A	CBA 925 A-BANI A																											

Yasmaḫ-Adad	1	2	3	4	5	6	7	8	9	10	11	12	13	14	15	16	17	18	19	20	21	22	23	24	25	26	27	28	29	30
Aḫi-Aya			CBA 980 Ac																											
Unknown limu/year		11:44 E		11:44 E	11:44 E			1:133 E																						1:10 E
Unknown limu/year +day																														
Unknown day	CBA 922 A.BANI A	CBA 965 A.BANI Ac																												

Yasmaḫ-Adad	1	2	3	4	5	6	7	8	9	10	11	12	13	14	15	16	17	18	19	20	21	22	23	24	25	26	27	28	29	30
Ašur-Malik (#1)																														
Awīliya (#2)																														
Addu-bani/ Census (#3)																														
Asqudum (#4)																														
Ennam-Ašur (#5)																														
Ḫali-Malik (#6)																														
Ikupiya (#7)																														
Ikūn-pī-Sin (#8)																														
Ili-ellati (#9)																														
Ibni-Addu (#10)																														
Murikmānu/Rikmānu (#11)																														
Nimar-Sin/ Nimer-Sin (#12)																							[VII:10] A							
Puṣṣanum (#13)																														
Šalim-Ašar A (#14)																														
Šalim-Ašar B (#15)																														
Ṭāb-ṣilli-Ašur (#16)																														
Ṭāb-ṣilli-Ašur II (#17)																														
Nergal (date-year)																														

Yasmaḫ-Adad	1	2	3	4	5	6	7	8	9	10	11	12	13	14	15	16	17	18	19	20	21	22	23	24	25	26	27	28	29	30
Aḫi-Aya																														
Unknown limu/year															I:8 II:8 E E					IV:78 E										
Unknown limu/year +day																														
Unknown day	CBA 946 A-BANI A	CBA 952 A-BANI A	CBA 936 A-BANI Ac																											

Yasmaḫ-Adad	1	2	3	4	5	6	7	8	9	10	11	12	13	14	15	16	17	18	19	20	21	22	23	24	25	26	27	28	29	30
Ašur-Malik (#1)																														
Awīliya (#2)																														
Addu-bani/ Census (#3)	CBA 973 CBA 979 A/P A									CBA 942 A																				
Asqudum (#4)																														
Ennam-Ašur (#5)																														
Ḫali-Malik (#6)																														
Ikupiya (#7)																														
Ikūn-pī-Sin (#8)																														
Ili-ellati (#9)			[CBA 387] Fc/tx																											
Ibni-Addu (#10)																														
Murikmānu/Rikmānu (#11)																														
Nimar-Sin/ Nimer-Sin (#12)																														
Puṣṣanum (#13)																														
Šalim-Ašar A (#14)																														
Šalim-Ašar B (#15)																														
Ṭāb-ṣilli-Ašur (#16)	VII:81 Ao/																													
Ṭāb-ṣilli-Ašur II (#17)	VII:78 :79 :80 Ao/P, R, K					VII:82 Ao/P	VII:83 Ao/R																							
Nergal (date-year)																														

Yasmaḫ-Adad	1	2	3	4	5	6	7	8	9	10	11	12	13	14	15	16	17	18	19	20	21	22	23	24	25	26	27	28	29	30
Aḫi-Aya	CBA 939 A																													
Unknown limu/year			CBA 387 AN.ŠEŠ.HU A																	1:26 E/t		VIII:7 L			1:65 E/R					
Unknown limu/year +day	1:88 E	IV:14 E																												
Unknown day	CBA 930 A-BANI A	CBA 993 A-BANI Ac/p																												

Yasmah-Adad	1	2	3	4	5	6	7	8	9	10	11	12	13	14	15	16	17	18	19	20	21	22	23	24	25	26	27	28	29	30
Ahi-Aya																														
Unknown limu/year																									11.10 E	1:39 :90 E E				
Unknown limu/year +day																														
Unknown day	CBA 986 A. MALIK Ae																													

Yasmaḫ-Adad

	1	2	3	4	5	6	7	8	9	10	11	12	13	14	15	16	17	18	19	20	21	22	23	24	25	26	27	28	29	30
Ašur-Malik (#1)																														
Awīliya (#2)										CBA 960 CBA 944 Ac Ac/p																				
Addu-bani/ Census (#3)										CBA 933 937 943 A Ap Ac																				
Asqudum (#4)																														
Ennam-Ašur (#5)																														
Ḫali-Malik (#6)																														
Ikupiya (#7)																														
Ikūn-pī-Sin (#8)																														
Ili-ellati (#9)																														
Ibni-Addu (#10)																														
Murikmānu/Rikmānu (#11)																														
Nimar-Sin/ Nimer-Sin (#12)																														
Puṣṣanum (#13)																														
Šalim-Ašar A (#14)																														
Šalim-Ašar B (#15)																														
Ṭāb-ṣilli-Ašur (#16)																														
Ṭāb-ṣilli-Ašur II (#17)											IX 1 A																			
Nergal (date-year)																														

X TAMḪĪRUM (2)

Yasmah-Adad	1	2	3	4	5	6	7	8	9	10	11	12	13	14	15	16	17	18	19	20	21	22	23	24	25	26	27	28	29	30
Ahi-Aya																						#314 [RUMA#] F/A								
Unknown limu/year																				[IV:78] E	V:59 E									
Unknown limu/year +day																														
Unknown day	CBA 987 A-BANI Ac/p	IRAQ 35 p175 [tell-TAYA] L	VIII:52 A-AYA LL																											

Yasmaḫ-Adad	1	2	3	4	5	6	7	8	9	10	11	12	13	14	15	16	17	18	19	20	21	22	23	24	25	26	27	28	29	30
Ašur-Malik (#1)																														
Awīliya (#2)																														
Addu-bani/ Census (#3)	CBA 929 948 967 A Ac Aa																													
Asqudum (#4)																														
Ennam-Ašur (#5)																														
Ḫali-Malik (#6)																														
Ikupiya (#7)	CBA 379 Ac																													
Ikūn-pī-Sin (#8)																														
Ili-ellati (#9)																														
Ibni-Addu (#10)																														
Murikmānu/Rikmānu (#11)																														
Nimar-Sin/ Nimer-Sin (#12)																														
Puṣṣanum (#13)																														
Šalim-Ašar A (#14)																														
Šalim-Ašar B (#15)																														
Ṭāb-ṣilli-Ašur (#16)																														
Ṭāb-ṣilli-Ašur II (#17)																														
Nergal (date-year)																														

Yasmaḫ-Adad	1	2	3	4	5	6	7	8	9	10	11	12	13	14	15	16	17	18	19	20	21	22	23	24	25	26	27	28	29	30
Aḫi-Aya																														
Unknown limu/year																														
Unknown limu/year +day																														
Unknown day	CBA 988 [989] A-BANI Ac/p	CBA 958 A-BANI A	CBA 992 A-BANI Ac/p																											

Yasmaḫ-Adad	1	2	3	4	5	6	7	8	9	10	11	12	13	14	15	16	17	18	19	20	21	22	23	24	25	26	27	28	29	30
Ašur-Malik (#1)																														
Awīliya (#2)														CBA 975 / 976 A A																
Addu-bani/ Census (#3)	CBA 977 Ac																						CBA 954 A/R							
Asqudum (#4)																														
Ennam-Ašur (#5)																														
Ḫali-Malik (#6)																														
Ikupiya (#7)																														
Ikūn-pī-Sin (#8)																														
Ili-ellati (#9)																														
Ibni-Addu (#10)																														
Murikmānu/Rikmānu (#11)																														
Nimar-Sin/ Nimer-Sin (#12)																														
Puṣṣanum (#13)																														
Šalim-Ašar A (#14)																														
Šalim-Ašar B (#15)																														
Ṭāb-ṣilli-Ašur (#16)																														
Ṭāb-ṣilli-Ašur II (#17)																														
Nergal (date-year)																														

Yasmah-Adad	1	2	3	4	5	6	7	8	9	10	11	12	13	14	15	16	17	18	19	20	21	22	23	24	25	26	27	28	29	30
Ahi-Aya																														
Unknown limu/year			CBA 994 [Awiliya] Ac									1:37 IV:80 E E				1:50 E				RA 7 p151-157 E	IV:76 E									
Unknown limu/year +day																														
Unknown day	CBA 931 A-BANI Ac	CBA 940 A-BANI A	CBA 951 A-BANI A	CBA 969 A-BANI A	CBA 970 A-BANI Ac	CBA 961 A-BANI A																								

(DIRIG.GA) (2) (Intercalary)

Yasmah-Adad

	1	2	3	4	5	6	7	8	9	10	11	12	13	14	15	16	17	18	19	20	21	22	23	24	25	26	27	28	29	30
Ahi-Aya																														
Unknown limu/year																			1;70 E											
Unknown limu/year +day																														
Unknown day																														

Yasmaḫ-Adad	1	2	3	4	5	6	7	8	9	10	11	12	13	14	15	16	17	18	19	20	21	22	23	24	25	26	27	28	29	30
Ašur-Malik (#1)																														
Awīliya (#2)																														
Addu-bani/ Census (#3)																														
Asqudum (#4)																														
Ennam-Ašur (#5)																														
Ḫali-Malik (#6)																														
Ikupiya (#7)																														
Ikūn-pī-Sin (#8)																														
Ili-ellati (#9)																														
Ibni-Addu (#10)																														
Murikmānu/Rikmānu (#11)																														
Nimar-Sin/ Nimer-Sin (#12)																														
Puṣṣanum (#13)																														
Šalim-Ašar A (#14)																														
Šalim-Ašar B (#15)																														
Ṭāb-ṣilli-Ašur (#16)																														
Ṭāb-ṣilli-Ašur II (#17)																														
Nergal (date-year)																				VIII:40 LL										

Zimri-Lim

	1	2	3	4	5	6	7	8	9	10	11	12	13	14	15	16	17	18	19	20	21	22	23	24	25	26	27	28	29	30
Euphrates (#29)																														
Benjaminites (#6)				XII:68 Fms	XII:69 Fms	XII:70 Ft		XI:34 Fms		XII:71 F	XII:72 F	XII:73 F	XII:74 F					XII:75 F	XII:76 F	XII:77 F	XI:35 Fm		XII:78 F	XI:36 Fc		XII:79 F		XII:80= XI:37 F F	XII:81? :82 F	XI:38 F
Benjaminites II (#7)												S143 p36 A																		
Aš̌lakka (#2)				VIII:71 L																XI:15 A	VIII:76 L						XII:19 F.A.			
Aš̌lakka II (#3)																			IX:7 A											
Throne of Šamaš (#16)										[VII:105] AR	VII:106 Ap									XVIII:62 Ap						S143:69 [XVIII p109] A	XII:189 XII:190 Fc Fc			
Throne of Šamaš II (#17)																														
Census (#26)	IX:105 [IX:109] Fm F	XII:404 Fm			XII:405 :406 Fm Fc	XII:407 Fc		IX:106 F		XII:408 Fm		XII:409 Fm	XI:175 Fm	XII:410 :411 Fm Fc	XI:177 Fc	XII:412 Rk	IX:107 (?) Fm	VII:134 IX:106 Fm Fo	[XII:413] Fm	XII:414 Fm	IX:108 A	XII:415 Fm		XII:416 Fm	VII:135 A	XII:417 [IX:128] Fm Fm	VII:282 F	XI:178 Fm		→
Dūr Yaḫdun-Lim (#28)	S52:8 [XVIII:105] XI:220 F F		XII:535 F	XII:536 XI:221 F Fc	XI:222 F	IX:169 A	XII:537 Fm		XII:538 F			[XII:542] Fm			IX:170 Fm		XII:539 Fm	VII:154 F	XI:223 Fm	XII:540 F	XII:541 F	[XII:542] Fm	XI:224 XII:543 F Rk		XII:544 F	XI:225 XII:545 F F	XI:225 F			
Ḫatta (#21)	XI:127 Rk	XII:306 IX:56 F FAm				XII:307 XI:128 F Fo		XII:308 F			XII:309 F	XII:310 XII:311 F F			IX:57 F	IX:58 Fo	IX:59 F			XI:129 F	VIII:56 Ll		VII:120 Ap	XI:139 Fo	XII:313 F	XI:131 F		XII:314 F	VII:109 IX:60 F A	
Ḫatta II (#21b)			XI:149 Fc																											
Elam Expedition (#13)	SYRIA 55 p.335 A								VIII:66 L		IX:29 Ap									IX:30 A										IX:30 A
Addu of Maḫanum (#18)																								SYRIA 55p342 A						
Babylon (#11)				XVIII:108 A						IX:18 (?) A																				
Babylon II (#12)																														
Throne of Dagan (#14)										[VII:105] AR												S52:11 =XVIII p108 A								
Throne of Dagan II (#15)							SYRIA 55p.339																							
IInd Aš̌lakka (#3b)																													SYRIA 55, p.335 (S.1084 888)	

Zimri-Lim

	1	2	3	4	5	6	7	8	9	10	11	12	13	14	15	16	17	18	19	20	21	22	23	24	25	26	27	28	29	30
Throne of his Father (#1)																														
Kaḫat (#4)																														
Kaḫat II (#4b)																		SYRIA 55 p339						SYRIA 55 p343 n.2						
Mišlān (#5)																														
Elam Victory (#8)																														
Elaḫut Victory (#9)																														
Qarni-Lim (#10)																														
IInd Babylon (#12b)																														
Throne of Diritum (#19)																														
Addu of Halab (#20)																														
Annunitum of Šeḫrum (#22)																														
Addu of Appan (#23)																														
Addu of Appan II (#24)																														
Lions of Dagan (#25)																														
Šaramā (#27)																														
Ḫabur (#30)																														
Muballitum (#31)	[IX:217] F →						XII:616 XII:617 F Am →	VII:179 F	[IX:217] F →	XII:618 F	XI:255 F		XII:619 Fc		XII:620 F	XII:621 Fc →		[IX:217] F →		XII:622 .623 R? F	XII:625 IX:198 F F	XII:626 F	→		XII:627 [IX:217] F →				XII:628 F	[IX:217 V:25-29] Rk →
Yamḫad (#32)																														

I URĀḪUM (3)

Zimri-Lim

	1	2	3	4	5	6	7	8	9	10	11	12	13	14	15	16	17	18	19	20	21	22	23	24	25	26	27	28	29	30
Andariq (#33!)																														
Unknown year	IX:218 VII:192 R_K A							XII:737 IX:218 → A F_{MS}						[VIII:54] XII:669 Lℓ F	XII:670 :730 VIII:566 F Lℓ A	XIII:82-3 XI:274 XII:681 Etk Rk Rk	XIII:84 :85 Etk F	XIII:86 IX:218 Etk F		XI:273 F		[IX:218] F!		XII:642 :716 F F_o		VII:107 A	IX:277 AF_o			
Unknown year and day	VII:105 AR	IX:227 F	VII:298 A		IX:222 F	IX:230 F/A	IX:206 F	XIII:87 Lt	XII:680 [IX:218: IV:46] F_c																					
Unknown day	XII:547 = IX:224 D-Y-L F	XII:546 D-Y-L F	IX:223 [ŠAMAŠ] F	IX:217 MUBAL F	XII:83 BENJ F	XII:84 BENJ F_S	IX:11 AŠLAKKA F	IX:120 CENSUS F_O	VII:281 ḪATTA A																					
Census II (#26b)									Syrie 55, p. 343 n. 29																					

II MALKĀNUM (1)

Zimri-Lim

	1	2	3	4	5	6	7	8	9	10	11	12	13	14	15	16	17	18	19	20	21	22	23	24	25	26	27	28	29	30
Euphrates (#29)																														
Benjaminites (#6)	XII:85 RK	XII:86 F	XII:87 Fm				XII:89 F	XII:90 F	XII:91 F	XII:92 F	XII:93 F			XII:94 F		XI:39 XII:96 F Rk	XII:97 F			XII:98 F										
Benjaminites II (#7)																														
Ašlakka (#2)		XI:16 Am			XI:17 F																									
Ašlakka II (#3)																XI:70 Fms ↓										VIII:94 L				
Throne of Šamaš (#16)		XII:191 [IX:219] → Fc Fms					XI:108 [IX:219] R Fms		[IX:219] Fms	[VIII:26] → Ll		XI:69 Fc				XI:71 XII:192 :193 Fc Fo Rk	[IX:219] → Fms		XI:72 XII:194 Fo Fms	XII:195 Fc	IX:41 Fo		S215 p189 =XVII p109 A	XVIII:45 A	XII:197 XII:196 Fo Fms	XII:198 Fms		XII:73 Fo		
Throne of Šamaš II (#17)			Syria 55, p.343 n.2.																											
Census (#26)	XII:418 [IX:114] → Rk Rk				XI:179 Fm	XII:419 Fm		XII:420 Fm	XI:180 Fm	IX:110 Fm		XII:421 Fm			XII:422 Fm	IX:112 A	IX:111 Fm				XI:181 [IX:114] → Fm		XI:182 Fm	XII:423 :424 Fo Fm	XI:183 → Ft		XII:425 [IX:214] → Fm		IX:113 Fm	
Dūr Yaḫdun-Lim (#28)	XII:549 XI:226 XII:548 Fc Rkm Fc	XII:550 F		XII:551 A	XII:552 A		XII:553 :554 IX:171 Fc E F	XII:555 Fc	XII:556 Fc			XII:557 F	VII:155= XII:559 :558 Fc F	XI:227 :228 F F		XII:560 :561 F Rk			XI:229 F											
Ḫatta (#21)	IX:61 [IX:71] → F Ft	XII:315 F	IX:62 Fo		IX:63 F	XII:316 F	XII:317 F	XII:318 F		XII:319 F	IX:64 F	IX:65 F		XI:132 XII:320 :321 Fc F F	IX:66 F	IX:67 F	IX:68 F		IX:69 A						IX:70 A					
Ḫatta II (#21b)																														
Elam Expedition (#13)						[XII:110] Fo										[XII:110] Fo										[XII:110] Fo				
Addu of Maḫanum (#18)										[VIII:26] Ll																				
Babylon (#11)																IX, p.267 F														
Babylon II (#12)																														
Throne of Dagan (#14)										[VIII:26] Ll																				
Throne of Dagan II (#15)																														
IInd Ašlakka (#3b)																														

Zimri-Lim

	1	2	3	4	5	6	7	8	9	10	11	12	13	14	15	16	17	18	19	20	21	22	23	24	25	26	27	28	29	30
Throne of his Father (#1)																														
Kaḫat (#4)																														
Kaḫat II (#4b)																														
Mišlān (#5)																					IX:12 A									
Elam Victory (#8)																														
Elaḫut Victory (#9)																														
Qarni-Lim (#10)																														
IInd Babylon (#12b)																														
Throne of Diritum (#19)																														
Addu of Halab (#20)																														
Annunitum of Šehrum (#22)										VIII:10 L																				
Addu of Appan (#23)																														
Addu of Appan II (#24)																														
Lions of Dagan (#25)																														
Šaramā (#27)																														
Ḫabur (#30)																														
Muballittum (#31)	[IX:193] Rk/F.	F→					XII:629 :630 F F	→	→	XII:631 F	XII:632 F	[IX:193]	XII:633 F →	IX:194 F	XII:634 F	XI:256 F	[IX:193] →	→	XII:635 F	XI:257 F				[IX:193] →	→	IX:195 F			[IX:193] →	→
Yamḫad (#32)																														

II MALKĀNUM (3)

Zimri-Lim

	1	2	3	4	5	6	7	8	9	10	11	12	13	14	15	16	17	18	19	20	21	22	23	24	25	26	27	28	29	30
Andariq (#33!)																														
Unknown year	IX:71 [HATTA?] F			XII:671 F				XI:275 F							IX:270 A	XII:729 F	XII:688 Fc	[XII:690] Fc →	XIII:88 A	XII:689 Fc				XIV:23 E				[XII:690] Fc		
Unknown year and day		IX:222 F				IX:260 A	IX:267 A	XI:276 F	XI:277 F	XII:643 :644 F F	VII:301	VII:263 A	XVIII:63 A	RA 72 187 n.6 A?																
Unknown day	VII:110 HATTA A	XII:199 ŠAMAŠ F	XII:426 CENSUS Fm	XII:562 D-Y-L Fc	IX:234 [CENSUS] F	XII:88 BENJ Fm	XII:95 BENJ F	XII:110 EL.EX. Fo	IX:120 CENSUS Fo	IX:71 [HATTA] Rk	[XII:449] CENSUS Fc	IX:219 [ŠAMAŠ] Rkm																		
Census II (#26b)																														

Zimri-Lim

	1	2	3	4	5	6	7	8	9	10	11	12	13	14	15	16	17	18	19	20	21	22	23	24	25	26	27	28	29	30
Euphrates (#29)																														
Benjaminites (#6)							XII:99 F	XI:40 F		XII:100 F	XII:101 F	XI:41 F			XII:102 F					XVIII:69 A/R		XII:103 F					XI:42 F/T			
Benjaminites II (#7)																														
Ašlakka (#2)																														
Ašlakka II (#3)			S. 160.55 XVIII;105 A ↓																								RA 72 187 n.6 A?			
Throne of Šamaš (#16)	XVIII:46 A	XII:200 :201 F_{ms} F	XI:74 XII:202 F_t F	XII:203 F_c				XI:75 F_c						XI:76 F	XII:204 F_o		XII:205 F_o			XI:77 F_{co}	XI:78 F_o		XII:206 F_c				XI:79 XII:207 F_c F_{ms}	XI:80 S52:175 =XVIII:105 F_o A		
Throne of Šamaš II (#17)																														
Census (#26)	XII:427 F_o				IX:234 =XI:184 F_c/t				SYRIA 55, p.334		IX:234 F_c											XII:429 XII:428 F_m F_o	XI:185 IX:115 F_m A		IX:116 F_m	[IX:128] F_m				
Dūr Yahdun-Lim (#28)						XII:563 F			[XII:567] VII:157 VII:156 F A Ap	XII:564 F	IX:172 F		XII:565 F		XI:230 F	XI:231 Rk	XII:566 F	[VIII:31] Ll	[XII:567] [VIII:31+725] F LL		XII:568 F	XII:569 =XI:232 XII:570 XII:571 F_c F F_o	XII:572 F	VII:158 XII:573 F R/F			XI:233 F	IX:173 [TOTAL] Rk/F		XI:234 F
Hatta (#21)				St. MAR. p. 48:13 R	XI:133 F			XI:134 F	XII:322 :323 F F_o			XII:324 F				XI:135 F				XII:325 :326 F F_o	XII:327 F	IX:72 F		XI:136 F	[IX:73] F_o	[IX:73] F_o				
Hatta II (#21b)																														
Elam Expedition (#13)							XII:111 F	XII:112 F_o	XI:49 F	XII:113 :114 F																			XI:50 F_c	
Addu of Mahanum (#18)																														
Babylon (#11)																														
Babylon II (#12)																							SYRIA 55, p.340						SYRIA 55, p.343 n.2	
Throne of Dagan (#14)																														
Throne of Dagan II (#15)																														
IInd Ašlakka (#3b)																											[illegible]			

Zimri-Lim	1	2	3	4	5	6	7	8	9	10	11	12	13	14	15	16	17	18	19	20	21	22	23	24	25	26	27	28	29	30
Throne of his Father (#1)																														
Kaḫat (#4)																														
Kaḫat II (#4b)																														
Mišlān (#5)																														
Elam Victory (#8)																														
Elaḫut Victory (#9)																														
Qarni-Lim (#10)																														
IInd Babylon (#12b)																														
Throne of Diritum (#19)																														
Addu of Halab (#20)																														
Annunitum of Šeḫrum (#22)																						VII:124 A								
Addu of Appan (#23)																														
Addu of Appan II (#24)																														
Lions of Dagan (#25)																														
Šaramā (#27)																														
Ḫabur (#30)																														
Muballittum (#31)																														
Yamḫad (#32)																														

Zimri-Lim

	1	2	3	4	5	6	7	8	9	10	11	12	13	14	15	16	17	18	19	20	21	22	23	24	25	26	27	28	29	30
Andariq (#33!)																									VII:258 A ↓					
Unknown year	IX:220 Fm			XIII:89 E/Gn	IX:221 Fm	IX:221 Fm				VIII:31 Ll				XII:645 :691 F Fc				XIII:90 XI:278 T F	VIII:31+ 71c Ll	VII:250 [VIII:48] F Ll		XII:672 Fms		XIII:91- :94 E/Gn	VII:250 [VII:225 =226] F A →	→	XIV:104 E →	→	→	
Unknown year and day	IX:226 F	IX:199 Ft	VIII:51 Ll	IX:225 Rk	XII:646 F	XII:647 F	XI:280 Fc	XI:279 Rk	XII:735 A	XII:738 F/R	XII:705 :706 F	SYRIA 55, p.354	IX:221 Rk	VII:258 A																
Unknown day	IX:128? CENSUS F	IX:120 CENSUS Fo	IX:233 [CENSUS] F	VII:263	XII:574 D-Y-L F	VII:159 D-Y-L	XII:208 ŠAMAŠ Fm	IX:117 CENSUS Fm	XI:186 CENSUS Fm	XII:428 CENSUS Fo	XII:430 CENSUS Rk	IX:19 BABYLON A	IX:20 BABYLON A	VII:111 HATTA F	IX:74 HATTA Fo	XI:137 HATTA F	XI:138 HATTA F	[XII:449] CENSUS Fc												
Census II (#26b)																														

Zimri-Lim	1	2	3	4	5	6	7	8	9	10	11	12	13	14	15	16	17	18	19	20	21	22	23	24	25	26	27	28	29	30
Euphrates (#29)															VIII:61 Ll					VII:178 Fc										
Benjaminites (#6)													XII:104 Fc/T																	
Benjaminites II (#7)																														
Aŝlakka (#2)																														
Aŝlakka II (#3)																														
Throne of Šamaš (#16)	XI:81 XII:209 :210 Fm Fo Rk			XII:211 F	VII:12 Fo				XI:82 Fm									VII:13 Fo	XII:212 RA 69,27 Fs R/Fo	XII:213 Fm					XII:215 :214 Fms Fms	XII:216 F	XII:217 XVIII:44 Fo A	XII:218? VII:257? Fo A	XII:218? Fo	XII:219 XVIII:47 :48 Fo A
Throne of Šamaš II (#17)																														
Census (#26)	XII:431 Rk			XII:432 Rk		XII:433 Fc	XII:434 :435 Fo Fo		XII:436 :437 Fm Rk		XII:438 Fm		XI:187 Fc/A		XII:439 Fo		XII:440 F/A	[IX:121] → F		XII:441 Fm				IX:118 Fm			XII:442 Fm	IX:119 Fm		VII:136 A
Dūr Yaḫdun-Lim (#28)	XII:575 Fc	VII:160 A			VII:161 XII:576 A Fo	XI:235 Fc	IX:174 F	XI:236 Fc	IX:175 Fc/A		XII:577 F/R	XI:237 Fc	XI:238 Fo	XI:239 XII:578 Fc Fc		XI:240 F/R		XII:579 Fo										XII:580 XI:24 Fo F		
Ḫatta (#21)			XII:329 F	IX:75 Fo		XII:330 F	XII:331 F		XI:139 F	IX:76 F	XII:332 F	XII:333 F	XII:334 Fo	XII:335 F		XII:336 F	VIII:32 Ll	VII:112 Ap	XII:337 F	IX:77 [IX:80] A/R A		XII:339 Fo				XII:340 F	XII:341 F	IX:78 Fo	IX:79 F	XII:342 [IX:80] Rk
Ḫatta II (#21b)																														
Elam Expedition (#13)		XII:115 Fc		VII:92 A														XII:116 F	VII:93 XII:117 Ll F			XII:118 :119 F F		XI:51 XII:120 F Fc			XI:52 F		XII:121 F	
Addu of Maḫanum (#18)																														
Babylon (#11)								VIII:23 Ll		VII:89 Fc																				
Babylon II (#12)																														
Throne of Dagan (#14)																														
Throne of Dagan II (#15)																														
IInd Aŝlakka (#3b)	VIII:74 (?) Ll																													

Zimri-Lim

	1	2	3	4	5	6	7	8	9	10	11	12	13	14	15	16	17	18	19	20	21	22	23	24	25	26	27	28	29	30
Throne of his Father (#1)																														
Kaḫat (#4)																														
Kaḫat II (#4b)																														
Mišlān (#5)																														
Elam Victory (#8)																														
Elaḫut Victory (#9)																														
Qarni-Lim (#10)																														
IInd Babylon (#12b)	[IX:24] Ap		IX:25=26 Ap																					IX:27 Ap						
Throne of Diritum (#19)																														
Addu of Halab (#20)																														
Annunitum of Šehrum (#22)																														
Addu of Appan (#23)																														
Addu of Appan II (#24)																														
Lions of Dagan (#25)																														
Šaramā (#27)																														
Ḫabur (#30)	VIII:24 Ll																													
Muballitṭum (#31)																														
Yamḫad (#32)																						VIII:79 Ll								

Zimri-Lim

	1	2	3	4	5	6	7	8	9	10	11	12	13	14	15
Andariq (#33!)	VII:258 A ↓			VII:258 A ↓		1:67 E ↓									
Unknown year	VII:225 :226 IX:24 A Ap A	VII:230 A		VII:250 :225 :226 F A A	VII:259 III:79 A E	XII:673 S.143.123 =XVIII p105 F A	VII:225= :226! IX:201 A Rk	1:5 E		VII:228 A	IX:221 Fm	XI:281 XII:732 Fc/R F		VII:258 A	IX:221 XIII:95 IX:255 F A Etx
Unknown year and day	XII:449 F	IX:226 F	VII:226 A	IX:122 F/A	VIII:29 Lt	VIII:36 Lt	XII:736 F	XII:706 F	VIII:27 Lt	IX:200 F	VIII:47 Lt	VIII:39 Lt	VI:76 E	XIII:139 Lt	VIII:29 Lt
Unknown day	XII:338 HATTA F	IX:80 HATTA A	VIII:33 [HATTA] Lt	IX:122 CENSUS F	XII:122 EL.EX. F	S.160.18 =XVIII p.109 ŠAMAŠ A	VIII:22-3 [DAGAN] Lt					RA 69, 25 DAGAN Fo/R	IX:120 CENSUS Fo	XII:449 CENSUS Fc	VIII:32 [ELAM] Lt
Census II (#26b)															

	16	17	18	19	20	21	22	23	24	25	26	27	28	29	30
Andariq (#33!)			VII:258 A ↓												
Unknown year	IX:221 1:19 Fm E	IX:221 Fm	VII:226? IX:221 A Fm	VII:226? IX:221 A Fm	VII:226 A	XII:692 Fc	VII:225 :226 A A	VII:226 XIII:96 A Etx	VII:226 IX:221 A Fm	IX:221 XI:282 11:8 Fm E F/A			IX:220 VII:237 Fm A		IX:221 11:8 Fm E
Unknown year and day	VIII:33 Lt	IX:200 F													
Unknown day	VIII:74 [???] Lt	VIII:24 [??] Lt													
Census II (#26b)															

Zimri-Lim

	1	2	3	4	5	6	7	8	9	10	11	12	13	14	15	16	17	18	19	20	21	22	23	24	25	26	27	28	29	30
Euphrates (#29)																														
Benjaminites (#6)						XII:105 Fc																								
Benjaminites II (#7)																XI:48 Fc														
Aŝlakka (#2)																														
Aŝlakka II (#3)																S.215:322 XVIII p 109 A ↓														
Throne of Šamaš (#16)	XI:83 Fo	XII:220 S.215.312 (XVIII,109) Fo A		XII:222 Fms			XII:223 Fms	XVIII:48 A	IX:42 Fms	XII:225 Fo		XI:84 Fo	XI:85 Fc	XII:226 Fms	XII:228 :227 Fo Fms	XII:229 XI:86 F/c F			IX:42 Fm	VII:18 Fo	XII:230 Fo	VII:19 Fo	XII:231 232 Fms Fo	XI:87 XII:233 Fo Fo	XI:89 XII:234 XI:88 F Fm F		VII:20 Fo			XII:236 Fc
Throne of Šamaš II (#17)																														
Census (#26)	IX:123 Rk FR/F	XI:188 Fo F	XII:443 Fm F	XI:189 Fc F	←[IX:121]→ (cols. 1–10) F	XII:444 Fm F	F	XI:190 Fm F	XII:445 Fm F	F							XII:446 Fm	XII:447 Fm				XII:448 Fc							XI:191 Rp	
Dūr Yaḫdun-Lim (#28)	XI:242 F	XII:581 IX:176 Fo A/R		XI:243 XII:582 IX:177 F F/A Fo		XII:583 :584 [IX:178] Fo Lt Fo	XII:586 F	IX:179 F		VII:162 A			VIII:33c Ll	VIII:80 Ll		XII:585 Rk											S.143.3 =XVIII p 108 A	VII:163 A		XII:587 :588 Fo R/Fc
Ḫatta (#21)		XII:343 :344 F Fo	VII:113 XI:140 A Fc	XII:345 F	XI:141 F	IX:81 [IX:178] F Lt		IX:82 F	XII:346 F	VII:121 XII:347 A Fc		XII:348 XI:142 F Fo	XII:349 F	XII:350 F	VII:114 A															
Ḫatta II (#21b)																														
Elam Expedition (#13)		VII:94 F		XII:123 F		XII:124 F	IX:31 A			XII:125 F	VII:95 A			XII:126 Fo	XII:127 F				XII:128 F	XII:129 F				XI:53 F		IX:32 XII:130 F F		XII:132 :131 F Fo	XI:54 F	
Addu of Maḫanum (#18)																														
Babylon (#11)																														
Babylon II (#12)																														
Throne of Dagan (#14)					IX:36 A																								VII:98 Ll	
Throne of Dagan II (#15)																														
IInd Aŝlakka (#3b)					S.160.190 (= XXI) A	IX:8 A																								

V HIBIRTUM (2)

Zimri-Lim	1	2	3	4	5	6	7	8	9	10	11	12	13	14	15	16	17	18	19	20	21	22	23	24	25	26	27	28	29	30
Throne of his Father (#1)																														
Kaḫat (#4)																														
Kaḫat II (#4b)																														
Mišlān (#5)																														
Elam Victory (#8)																														
Elaḫut Victory (#9)																														
Qarni-Lim (#10)																														
IInd Babylon (#12b)																														
Throne of Diritum (#19)																														
Addu of Halab (#20)									IX:47 Fc																					
Annunitum of Šehrum (#22)																														
Addu of Appan (#23)																														
Addu of Appan II (#24)	VIII:28 Ll																													
Lions of Dagan (#25)																														
Šaramā (#27)																														
Ḫabur (#30)																														
Muballittum (#31)																														
Yamḫad (#32)	VIII:25 c. Ll																													

V HIBIRTUM (3)

Zimri-Lim

	1	2	3	4	5	6	7	8	9	10	11	12	13	14	15	16	17	18	19	20	21	22	23	24	25	26	27	28	29	30
Andariq (#33!)																														
Unknown year	IX:203 Rk	JCS. 21.M p.227 XII:693 E Fc	XI:283 XII:674 F F		XII:694 Fc					XII:725 → Fo	Fo	Fo	→	S 215:318 =XVIII p109 IX:282 A F								VIII:27 LL						XIII:99 Etx		
Unknown year and day	VIII:59 Ll	XI:284 F	XII:717 Fo	XII:707 Fo	VI:27 E																									
Unknown day	XII:235 ŠAMAŠ Fo	XI:107 ŠAMAŠ Fms	XII:224 ŠAMAŠ Fc	XII:221 ŠAMAŠ Fc	S215:312 =XVIII p109 ŠAMAŠ A	XII:589 D-Y-L F	XI:252 D-Y-L F	VII:164 D-Y-L A	XII:449 CENSUS Fc																					
Census II (#26b)																														

VI IGI.KUR (1)

Zimri-Lim

	1	2	3	4	5	6	7	8	9	10	11	12	13	14	15	16	17	18	19	20	21	22	23	24	25	26	27	28	29	30
Euphrates (#29)																														
Benjaminites (#6)																														
Benjaminites II (#7)																									XII:108 Rk					
Ašlakka (#2)																														
Ašlakka II (#3)																														
Throne of Šamaš (#16)			XII:237 Fms	[VII:108] XII:238 A Fo	VIII:71 L	XI:90 :91 Fms Fo	XVIII:49 XI:92 A F	IX:43 VII:22 Fc Fo		VII:23 XII:239 XI:93 Fo F/A Fc						XI:94 Rk		XVIII:41 A								IX:44 XI:9? Fc Fms				
Throne of Šamaš II (#17)																														
Census (#26)	XII:450 Fo/Rk									XII:451 Fo/A		XII:452 Fc/A				XII:453 Fo/Rk														
Dūr Yaḫdun-Lim (#28)	XII:590 IX:185 → Fo F	IX:180 A F	XII:591 F F	VII:165 Am F	XI:244 VII:166 F F A	XI:245 F F	F	XII:592 F F	RA64,34 A F	F	XII:593 F F	VII:167 A F	XII:594 F F →	XII:595 F		XI:246 F	VII:168 IX:185 → A F	XII:596 F F	IX:181 F F	IX:183 XII:597 IX:182 F Fc F F	F	F	XII:598 F F			XII:599 F		IX:185 F	IX:184 VII:169 Ap A	XII:600 Fo
Ḫatta (#21)				VII:115 :116 A A			VII:117 A			VII:117 A				VII:117 → A	A	A	A	A					VII:117 A			VII:117 A				VII:117 A
Ḫatta II (#21b)																														
Elam Expedition (#13)		XI:55 F	XII:133 F					XII:134 F	XII:135 F			IX:33 F/A																		
Addu of Maḫanum (#18)																														
Babylon (#11)																														
Babylon II (#12)																														
Throne of Dagan (#14)				[VII:108] A		IX:37 A	VII:99 A					S143:80 =XVIII,109 A					SYRIA 55p337?										SYRIA 55p337?			
Throne of Dagan II (#15)																														
IInd Ašlakka (#3b)																														

Zimri-Lim

	1	2	3	4	5	6	7	8	9	10	11	12	13	14	15	16	17	18	19	20	21	22	23	24	25	26	27	28	29	30
Throne of his Father (#1)																														
Kaḫat (#4)																														
Kaḫat II (#4b)																														
Mišlān (#5)																														
Elam Victory (#8)																														
Elaḫut Victory (#9)																														
Qarni-Lim (#10)																														
IInd Babylon (#12b)																														
Throne of Diritum (#19)																														
Addu of Halab (#20)																														
Annunitum of Šehrum (#22)																														
Addu of Appan (#23)																														
Addu of Appan II (#24)																														
Lions of Dagan (#25)																														
Šaramā (#27)																														
Ḫabur (#30)	VIII:24																													
Muballittum (#31)																														
Yamḫad (#32)																														

Zimri-Lim

	1	2	3	4	5	6	7	8	9	10	11	12	13	14	15	16	17	18	19	20	21	22	23	24	25	26	27	28	29	30
Andariq (#33!)																														
Unknown year	RA33,172 E				VII:204 RA33,172 A E	IX:241 F/A			IX:241 F/A	IX:241 F/A		III:5 IX:276 E A		IX:241 F/A		III:5 IX:241 E F	VIII:65 L											VII:303		
Unknown year and day	XII:707 F/A	IX:229 F	VIII:36 L	XII:718 Fo																										
Unknown day	XII:240 ŠAMAŠ Fc	VII:122 HATTA A	VIII:74 AŠK II Fc																											
Census II (#26b)																														

Zimri-Lim

	1	2	3	4	5	6	7	8	9	10	11	12	13	14	15	16	17	18	19	20	21	22	23	24	25	26	27	28	29	30
Euphrates (#29)																														
Benjaminites (#6)						XVIII:39 A																								
Benjaminites II (#7)																														
Ašlakka (#2)																														
Ašlakka II (#3)																														
Throne of Šamaš (#16)				XII:241 F/A				XII:242 Fc		XI:99 Fsm		XI:101 :100 Fc/o Fsm		XII:243 Fsm		XII:245 XI:102 :244 Fo RnFsm			XI:103 Fc				XII:246 Fs	XI:104 VII:103 Fsm/tFo	XII:247 XI:105 Fo Fsm	XII:248 Fsm	XI:106 Fsm	XII:249 Fsm		
Throne of Šamaš II (#17)																														[XII:460] Fo ↓
Census (#26)	XII:454 Rk/Fo													IX:125 XII:455 Fc Fc				XII:457 F		[XII:460] Fo						XI:195 [IX:234] Fc Fc		XII:458 Fms		IX:126 XII:459 VII:284 FmAFm
Dūr Yaḫdun-Lim (#28)	XII:601 Fc	IX:186 A/F					IX:187 A/F	XI:247 F	XII:602 F		XII:603 VII:286 F A	XII:604 VII:172 F A	[VII:173] A					[IX:188] A/p	[IX:188] A/p					XI:248 Fo	VII:174 Fo	XI:249 F	VII:175 F	XI:250 A/Ft	XII:605 XI:251 F/t Fc	XII:606 R
Ḫatta (#21)		VII:119 A																								XI:145 XII:351 Fo F			XII:352 F	XI:146 Fo
Ḫatta II (#21b)																														
Elam Expedition (#13)																														
Addu of Maḫanum (#18)					VIII:82 L																									
Babylon (#11)								VIII:23 L																				IX:22 A		VIII:89 A
Babylon II (#12)																														
Throne of Dagan (#14)		IX:38 A																												
Throne of Dagan II (#15)																														
IInd Ašlakka (#3b)																														

VII KINŪNUM (2)

Zimri-Lim	1	2	3	4	5	6	7	8	9	10	11	12	13	14	15	16	17	18	19	20	21	22	23	24	25	26	27	28	29	30
Throne of his Father (#1)																														
Kaḫat (#4)																														
Kaḫat II (#4b)																														
Mišlān (#5)																														
Elam Victory (#8)																														
Elaḫut Victory (#9)																														
Qarni-Lim (#10)																														
IInd Babylon (#12b)																														
Throne of Diritum (#19)																														
Addu of Halab (#20)													XII:265 Ap																	
Annunitum of Šehrum (#22)																														
Addu of Appan (#23)																														
Addu of Appan II (#24)																														
Lions of Dagan (#25)																														
Šaramā (#27)																														
Ḫabur (#30)																														
Muballittum (#31)																														
Yamḫad (#32)																														

Zimri-Lim

	1	2	3	4	5	6	7	8	9	10	11	12	13	14	15	16	17	18	19	20	21	22	23	24	25	26	27	28	29	30
Andariq (#33!)			IX:241 F/A ↓					XII:721 Fo ↓																						
Unknown year		XIII:37 E	I:53 [III:72] XI:287 E Fo E	XII:676 F			XIII:133 XII:719 E Fo	IX:262 XI:288 XII:720 A Fo Fo	VIII:29 L	IX:204 IV:35 F E		V:83 E		SYRIA 50:278 E				IX:249 XII:741 A A		IV:18 E						IX:234 F	IX:245 A			
Unknown year and day	IX:244 A	IX:246 A	IX:247 A	IX:248 A	II:6 [III:72] E E	IV:9 E	XII:648 Fm	XII:708 :709 F/A F/A																						
Unknown day	IX:188 D-Y-L A	IX:124 CENSUS A	XII:456 CENSUS Fc	XII:460 CENSUS Fo	IX:127 CENSUS A	[XI:45] BENJ. F	IX:234 [CENSUS] F																							
Census II (#26b)																														

VIII DAGAN (1)

Zimri-Lim

	1	2	3	4	5	6	7	8	9	10	11	12	13	14	15	16	17	18	19	20	21	22	23	24	25	26	27	28	29	30
Euphrates (#29)																														
Benjaminites (#6)								XII:106 Fc													XVIII: 67-68 AR						XI:43 Fsm	[XII:107] Fsm	[XII:107] Fsm	XI:44 F
Benjaminites II (#7)																				[XII:109] Fc										[XII:109] Fc
Aŝlakka (#2)																														IX:5 Fc/A
Aŝlakka II (#3)																														
Throne of Šamaš (#16)	XII:250 Fc				XII:251 Fc							XI:252 Fo	XI:253 Fo					[XII:254] Fc	[XII:254] Fc					XII:256 :257 :255 Fc Fsm Fc	XI:96 Fsm	XII:258 Fsm			XI:259 Fo	VII:102 XI:97 :98 A F Fo
Throne of Šamaš II (#17)																														
Census (#26)	XI:192 Fo/t					XI:193 IX:234 Fc Fc		IX:234 Fc		XII:462 :461 Fo Fc							VII:137 A				XII:463 Fm			VII:138 A	XII:464 Fo	XII:466 Ft		XI:194 Fo	XII:467 Fm	
Dūr Yaḫdun-Lim (#28)	XII:607 Fc								VII:170 IX:189 F A						VII:171 A				IX:190 Fc		IX:191 A/R									
Ḫatta (#21)						XI:143 XII:353 F Fo		XII:354 Fo		XII:355 F						VII:118 R/A						IX:83 F	XII:356 F		XI:144 F	XII:357 F	IX:84 A	XII:358 F		
Ḫatta II (#21b)																														
Elam Expedition (#13)																										VII:96 A				
Addu of Maḫanum (#18)		[IX:46] A													SYRIA 55, p.342 A															
Babylon (#11)																												VIII:91 Ax		
Babylon II (#12)																														
Throne of Dagan (#14)																														
Throne of Dagan II (#15)																														
IInd Aŝlakka (#3b)																														

Zimri-Lim

	1	2	3	4	5	6	7	8	9	10	11	12	13	14	15	16	17	18	19	20	21	22	23	24	25	26	27	28	29	30
Throne of his Father (#1)																														XII:6 F
Kaḫat (#4)																														
Kaḫat II (#4b)																														
Mišlān (#5)																														
Elam Victory (#8)																														
Elaḫut Victory (#9)																													IX, p. 267 F	
Qarni-Lim (#10)																														
IInd Babylon (#12b)																														
Throne of Diritum (#19)																														
Addu of Halab (#20)										XII:266 F_{sm}																				
Annunitum of Šehrum (#22)																						VIII:73 L<								
Addu of Appan (#23)																														
Addu of Appan II (#24)																														
Lions of Dagan (#25)																														
Šaramā (#27)																														
Ḫabur (#30)																														
Muballittum (#31)																														
Yamḫad (#32)																														

VIII DAGAN (3)

Zimri-Lim

	1	2	3	4	5	6	7	8	9	10	11	12	13	14	15	16	17	18	19	20	21	22	23	24	25	26	27	28	29	30
Andariq (#33!)																														
Unknown year	XII:722 Rk		XII:649 Fs	VII:85 Fo		XII:677 IX:234 Fs F	XII:678 Fsm	IX:234 F	XII:733 IX:269 F A	XII:679 T	XI:285 F	XII:650 T				[XII:723] Rk				II:78 E	IX:251 F/A		II:78 VII:84 E Fo		VIII:735 LL	XI:286 Fsm				
Unknown year and day	XII:703 F	XII:708 F/A	XII:734 F	IX:250 F	VIII:103 LC	VII:308 A																								
Unknown day	VII:283 CENSUS A	XII:468 CENSUS F	XI:113 ST. OF ADAD Fsm	XII:109 BEN. II F	IX:234 [CENSUS] Fc																									
Census II (#26b)																														

IX LILIATUM (1)

Zimri-Lim

	1	2	3	4	5	6	7	8	9	10	11	12	13	14	15
Euphrates (#29)															
Benjaminites (#6)	XII:20 Fsm		XII:21 Fsm	XII:22 Fsm	XI:18 Fsm	XI:19 Fsm	[XII:29] Fsm			XI:20 Fsm				XII:23 Fsm	
Benjaminites II (#7)															
Ašlakka (#2)															
Ašlakka II (#3)															
Throne of Šamaš (#16)	XI:56 :112 Fo Fc/R		XII:137 Fo	XII:138 Fo	XII:139 XI:57 Fo F	XII:140 Fo	VIII:49 Lℓ								
Throne of Šamaš II (#17)		[IX:89] Rk ↓													
Census (#26)	XI:150 F	IX:85 XII:361 [IX:90] Fm Rk Fo		XI:151 Fo			XII:362 :364 :363 Fo Fm Rk	XII:365 IX:86 Fo A/Fc		XI:152 Fm	IX p267 F	VIII:125 [XII:372] A Fm		XII:366 Fo	XII:367 Fm
Dūr Yaḫdun-Lim (#28)	XII:473 Rk		XII:474 :475 Fo F	XII:476 :477 F Fo	VII:141 IX:149 F A	XII:478 IX:149 Fo A	IX:131 XII:479 F/R Fo	XI:197 F	VII:142 F	IX:132 XII:480 :481 Fo Fc F	IX:133 F	IX:134 Fo	VII:143 XII:482 IX:149 Fo A Fc	IX:135 Fo	IX:136 XII:483 F Fo
Ḫatta (#21)	XII:267 = :268 Fs/R	XII:269 :270 = :271 Fs F/R F/R	[IX:212] → F	F	F	F	XII:272-3 :275 :274 F/R F/R F/R	F	F	F	F	F	IX:48 Ap	XII:276 [IX:212] ← F F	F
Ḫatta II (#21b)															
Elam Expedition (#13)															IHEB p187 A
Addu of Maḫanum (#18)															
Babylon (#11)															
Babylon II (#12)															
Throne of Dagan (#14)															
Throne of Dagan II (#15)															
IInd Ašlakka (#3b)															

	16	17	18	19	20	21	22	23	24	25	26	27	28	29	30
Euphrates (#29)															
Benjaminites (#6)		XII:24 Fsm	XI:21 F	S143:37= XVIII p105 A	XI:25 XVIII:69 F A		XII:26 Fsm	XVIII:55 :54 A A			XII:27 F	XII:28 F			XI:22 Fm
Benjaminites II (#7)															
Ašlakka (#2)		IX:2 XI:12 Fo A											XII:15 Fc		
Ašlakka II (#3)															
Throne of Šamaš (#16)	XI:58 Fsm	m.DUSSAUD p.993-4 [XII:141] Ap Fc	[XII:141] Fc	XII:142 Fsm		XII:143 F/t	XII:144 Fo	XI:60 :59 Fc Fsm							XII:147 Fo
Throne of Šamaš II (#17)															
Census (#26)	IX:87 XII:368 Fm [Fm]		VII:127 :126 A A	IX:88 XI:153 VII:128 Fo A Fm	XII:369 :370 F/t? Fo	XII:371 XI:154 Fm Fo	[XII:372] XI:155 Fm Fo	XII:373 VII:130 :129 Fm A A	XII:374 Fm	XII:375 VII:131 Fo A	XII:376 Fm				
Dūr Yaḫdun-Lim (#28)	IX:149 A	XII:484 F	IX:137 VII:144 F A	XI:198 :199 VII:145 F A Fc	VII:146 :147 F A	XII:485 :486 F Fo	XII:487 F	XII:488 F	XII:489 F	XI:200 F	IX:138 [F]	IX:139 F	XI:201 F	XII:490 F	
Ḫatta (#21)	XII:277 F F	IX:50 A F	F →	XII:278 F F	XII:279 F	XII:280 F		XII:281 [IX:212] → F F	XI:114 F F	F		[IX:212] → F	F	IX:51 A F	F
Ḫatta II (#21b)															
Elam Expedition (#13)															
Addu of Maḫanum (#18)														SYRIA 55 p342 A	
Babylon (#11)					IX:14 F				IX:15 F				RA 73 187 A		
Babylon II (#12)															
Throne of Dagan (#14)										IX:34 F					
Throne of Dagan II (#15)															
IInd Ašlakka (#3b)															

IX LILIATUM (2)

Zimri-Lim

	1	2	3	4	5	6	7	8	9	10	11	12	13	14	15	16	17	18	19	20	21	22	23	24	25	26	27	28	29	30
Throne of his Father (#1)																														
Kaḫat (#4)																														
Kaḫat II (#4b)																														
Mišlān (#5)																														
Elam Victory (#8)																														
Elaḫut Victory (#9)																														
Qarni-Lim (#10)																														
IInd Babylon (#12b)																														
Throne of Diritum (#19)																														
Addu of Halab (#20)																														
Annunitum of Šehrum (#22)																														
Addu of Appan (#23)																														
Addu of Appan II (#24)																														
Lions of Dagan (#25)																														
Šaramā (#27)																														
Ḫabur (#30)																														
Muballittum (#31)															vii:217 Lt															
Yamḫad (#32)																														

IX LILIATUM (3)

Zimri-Lim

	1	2	3	4	5	6	7	8	9	10	11	12	13	14	15
Andariq (#33!)															
Unknown year		XI:261 XIII:58-60 Fsm Lt	II:78 E						XII:657 Fm	XII:657 II:109 Fsm E	XII:658 Fm	XII:637 XIII:61 Fs Lt	XIII:100 Lt	IX:237 Fc	VII:217 At
Unknown year and day	XII:636 F	XI:259 IX:240 F/A F/A	XI:260 Fc	VII:297 A	VII:197 Ap	XII:636 F	XI:264 Fo	XI:263 Fc	XII:703 F	XII:727 F	VII:269 Lt	VII:273 Lt			
Unknown day	XI:156 CENSUS Rk	IX:89 CENSUS Rk	XII:146 ŠAMAS Fc	XII:145 ŠAMAŠ Fm	XI:107 ŠAMAŠ Fm	VII:91 BABYLON A	XI:23 BENJ. F	VII:87 BENJ. A	XVIII:56 BENJ. A	IX:240 [XI:259] [D-Y-L] F/A F/A	IX p 267 D-Y-L F	RA 69 p26 [S14] CENSUS R	IX:237 [ŠAMAŠ] Fc		
Census II (#26b)															

	16	17	18	19	20	21	22	23	24	25	26	27	28	29	30
Andariq (#33!)															
Unknown year	XI:262 A	VIII:90 Fc/A		VIII:97 Fc/A		[IX:21] → F	F	→ F	VIII:68 XII:659 L Fsm		[IX:21] → F	St. mar. p.43 A/R F	F	→ F	
Unknown year and day															
Unknown day															
Census II (#26b)															

X BĒLET-BĪRI (1)

Zimri-Lim

	1	2	3	4	5	6	7	8	9	10	11	12	13	14	15
Euphrates (#29)											VIII:62 L				
Benjaminites (#6)	XII:31 :30 XVIII:43 Ft A Rk	XII:32 F	XII:33 Ft	XII:34 Fm	XII:35 Fm		XII:36 Fsm	XII:37 Fsm	XII:38 Fm		XI:24 Ft		XVIII:57 A		
Benjaminites II (#7)															
Aškakka (#2)					XII:16 Fo				IX:3 Fm	[IX:9] Fo/A					[IX:10] F
Aškakka II (#3)															
Throne of Šamaš (#16)	XII:148 :149 Fm A/Fc	XI:61 Fo		XI:62 [IX:237] Fm Fc	XI:63 Fm			XII:151 Fo	XI:64 Fm/R						
Throne of Šamaš II (#17)															
Census (#26)	XII:377 Fo		S52:31= XVIII p105 A			XI:157 Fc			IX:91 Fo		XI:158 Fo	XI:159 Fo	XI:160 XII:378 Fo Fc	XII:381 :380 Fo Fm	XI:161 Fo
Dūr Yaḫdun-Lim (#28)		VII:148 XI:202 Fo F	XI:203 F	IX:140 F	XII:491 F	XI:204 F	XI:205 F	XII:492 Fo	XI:206 XII:493 Fo F				IX:141 :142 XII:494 Fc F F	[VII:149] XII:495 :496 Ap Fo F	XII:497 :498 Fo F
Ḫatta (#21)						IX:52 F		XII:282 Rk	XII:283 F	XI:116 F				XII:284 Fc	
Ḫatta II (#21b)															
Elam Expedition (#13)													IX:28 A		
Addu of Maḫanum (#18)															
Babylon (#11)															
Babylon II (#12)															
Throne of Dagan (#14)															
Throne of Dagan II (#15)															
IInd Aškakka (#3b)															

	16	17	18	19	20	21	22	23	24	25	26	27	28	29	30
Euphrates (#29)									VIII:87 L						
Benjaminites (#6)										XII:39 Fsm	XII:40 F		XII:41 Fsm		XVIII:58 -60 A-
Benjaminites II (#7)															
Aškakka (#2)				XIII:1 Ap											
Aškakka II (#3)															
Throne of Šamaš (#16)	XII:152 :164 Fc Fc			XI:153 Fsm										XI:65 Fm	
Throne of Šamaš II (#17)															
Census (#26)	XI:162 Fm	XII:382 Fo	[XI:164] :163 Fo Fm	XII:383 Fm	XII:384 Fo	XI:165 Fo		IX, p. 267 F	IX:92 Ft	IX:93 XI:166 F Fm	[XII:385] Fc			XII:386 Fm	
Dūr Yaḫdun-Lim (#28)	IX:143 XII:499 Fm Fk	XI:207 XII:500 Ft Fo	XII:501 F		XII:503 IX:144 XII:502 ApF Fo	XI:208 XII:504 [XI:265] Fo F/A F	VII:150 XII:505 Am F	XII:506 Fo	XII:507 [:508] F Fo	[XII:508] Fo	XII:509 Fo	XI:209 XII:510 F Fo	IX:145 F		XI:210 :211 :212 F Fo Fo
Ḫatta (#21)		IX:53 VIII:32 A Lt						XII:285 Fc							IX:54 Fo
Ḫatta II (#21b)															
Elam Expedition (#13)															
Addu of Maḫanum (#18)					XII:264 Fo										
Babylon (#11)										RA36, 48-49 A					
Babylon II (#12)															
Throne of Dagan (#14)															
Throne of Dagan II (#15)															
IInd Aškakka (#3b)															

X B̄ELET-B̄IRI (2)

Zimri-Lim

	1	2	3	4	5	6	7	8	9	10	11	12	13	14	15	16	17	18	19	20	21	22	23	24	25	26	27	28	29	30
Throne of his Father (#1)																														
Kaḫat (#4)																											RA 66, p. 132, 134 A			
Kaḫat II (#4b)																														
Mišlān (#5)																														
Elam Victory (#8)																														
Elaḫut Victory (#9)																														
Qarni-Lim (#10)																														
IInd Babylon (#12b)																														
Throne of Diritum (#19)																														
Addu of Halab (#20)																														
Annunitum of Šehrum (#22)																														
Addu of Appan (#23)																														
Addu of Appan II (#24)																														
Lions of Dagan (#25)																														
Šaramā (#27)																														
Ḫabur (#30)																														
Muballittum (#31)																														
Yamḫad (#32)																														

X BĒLET-BĪRI (3)

Zimri-Lim

	1	2	3	4	5	6	7	8	9	10	11	12	13	14	15	16	17	18	19	20	21	22	23	24	25	26	27	28	29	30
Andariq (#33!)																														
Unknown year		XVIII:52 A			XII:731 XIII:62 :63 F Etx Etx							XIV:31 XIII:64 E Etx	XII:660 XIII:65-69 Fm Etx			XIII:70 Etx				IX:196 F	XI:265 [D. Y-L] Ft					XIII:71 Etx	XI:266 RA 66,132 R K/t A		XII:662 Fm	
Unknown year and day	XI:267 F	XII:661 F	XII:638 Fsm	XII:701 F	XII:703 F	XII:727 F	IX:210 Ft	XII:736 F	IX:197 F																					
Unknown day	IX:94 CENSUS Fm	XII:378 CENSUS Fo	XII:155 ŠAMAŠ Fo	XII:150 ŠAMAŠ Fm	XII:547 ≃IX:224 CENSUS F/A	IX:240 [D-Y-L] F/A																								
Census II (#26b)																														

Zimri-Lim

	1	2	3	4	5	6	7	8	9	10	11	12	13	14	15	16	17	18	19	20	21	22	23	24	25	26	27	28	29	30
Euphrates (#29)																							VIII:69 L					XVIII:65=:70 A/R	XVIII:40 A	XVIII:66:53 A/R A
Benjaminites (#6)		XI:25 XII:42 Fm F	XII:43 F/A		[XII:44] F	[XII:44] F	XII:45 Fm			XII:46 F/R	XII:47 Fm	XII:48 Fsm		XVIII:61 A		XI:49 Fm	XI:26 F	[IX:213] → F	[XII:50] Fst F	XII:51 F	XII:52 Fm	XI:27 Fm	XII:53 Fm	[IX:213] → F	XI:28 Fsm F	XII:54 Fsm	XII:55 F			[IX:213] F
Benjaminites II (#7)																														
Aŝlakka (#2)								IX:4 Fc						XI:13 F/A													XII:17 Fc			
Aŝlakka II (#3)						[IX:237] Fc ↓																								
Throne of Šamaš (#16)	XII:156 Rk				XII:157 [IX:237] Fc Fc	XII:158 :164 IX:39 Fc Fc Fc		XII:159 Fc				[XII:160] Fo	[XII:160] Fo	XII:161 :164 Fc Fc	XII:162 Fo	XII:163 :164 [IX:237] Fs Fc Fc	XII:165 Fo			XII:166 Fs	XII:167 Fm		XII:168 Fo				XII:169 Fm	XII:170 Fm	XI:65 XII:171 Fm Fo	XII:172 Fm
Throne of Šamaš II (#17)				S 143:174 =XVIII:109 A ↓																										
Census (#26)	XII:387 [IX:98] → Fo Fm	S52:136= XVIII p108 A F	F	VII:132 [XII:388] A F F	XI:167 F F	F	IX:95 XI:168 Fm F Fm	F	F	F	F	IX:96 Fm F	S160:217= XVIII p105 A F	XI:169 XII:389 Fm F Fm	XII:390 F/t	[IX:98] → F	XII:391 Fm F	F	F	XII:392 IX:97 Fm F A	F	F	S52:5= XVIII p105 A F	[XII:393] Fm F	F	F	[XII:393] Fm F	XII:394 [XII:395] Fm F Fo	[XII:395] Fo F	[IX:98] R/K
Dūr Yaḫdun-Lim (#28)	XI:213 F	IX:146 F	IX:147 :149 F Am	XI:214 F	XII:511 F	XII:512 Fs	IX:148 XI:215 XII:513 F Fs Ft	XII:514 [IX:160] → F F	XII:515 F F	[IX:151] XI:216 F F Fc	IX:152 Fc F	XII:516 XII:517 F F	IX:153 Fc	IX:154 [IX:160] → F	XII:518 F		IX:155 XII:519 [IX:160] → F F Fo	XI:217 XII:520 F F	F	F	F	VII:151 F F	F	VII:152 IX:156 F F	[IX:157] F	F	IX:158 [IX:160] → F F	IX:159 F F	XII:521 F F	
Ḫatta (#21)	IX:55 [IX:212] → F F	[XII:286] F F	F F	XI:117 F	[IX:212] → F	F	F		XII:287 [IX:212] → F	F	XII:288 F	XII:289 :290 F F	[IX:212] → F	F	F	XI:118 Rk F	F			XI:119 F	[IX:212] → F	F	XII:291 F	F	F	XII:292 Ft		XII:293 Ft	XI:120 Ft	XI:121 XII:294 VII:120 F Ap Fo
Ḫatta II (#21b)																														
Elam Expedition (#13)																														
Addu of Maḫanum (#18)																														
Babylon (#11)																														
Babylon II (#12)																														
Throne of Dagan (#14)																													VII:97 A	
Throne of Dagan II (#15)																														
IInd Aŝlakka (#3b)																														

Zimri-Lim

	1	2	3	4	5	6	7	8	9	10	11	12	13	14	15	16	17	18	19	20	21	22	23	24	25	26	27	28	29	30
Throne of his Father (#1)																														
Kaḫat (#4)			[XIII:29] E					[X:142] E			[RA66, 132] E	RA66, 133 [X:142] Rp E			RA66, 133 R	[RA66, 133] R			[RA66, 134] A											RA49, [TEM.IV. viii] Ap
Kaḫat II (#4b)																														
Mišlān (#5)																														
Elam Victory (#8)																														
Elaḫut Victory (#9)																	RA66, p 135 R	RA66, p 135 R												
Qarni-Lim (#10)																														
IInd Babylon (#12b)																														
Throne of Diritum (#19)																														
Addu of Halab (#20)																														
Annunitum of Šehrum (#22)																														
Addu of Appan (#23)																														
Addu of Appan II (#24)																														
Lions of Dagan (#25)																														
Šaramā (#27)																														
Ḫabur (#30)																														
Muballittum (#31)																														
Yamḫad (#32)																														

Zimri-Lim

	1	2	3	4	5	6	7	8	9	10	11	12	13	14	15	16	17	18	19	20	21	22	23	24	25	26	27	28	29	30
Andariq (#33!)						SYRIA 19 p122 E ↓												IX:213 F ↓		IX:263 A ↓										
Unknown year		SYRIA 41 p 54 Fo	XIII:73? :72 :29 Etx Etx E	S.143:176 =XVIII,p109 A	IX:237 F	XII:663 IX:237? F F		XIII:74 X:142 Etx E	XI:268 XII:665 F Fsm	XII:666 IX:261 Fsm A	[& RA66 p.132] E E	X:142 RA66,119 E E		VII:208 XII:664 XIII:75 A Etx F	RA66,133 A	VIII:34 RA66,133 IX:237 L F E		XI:269 RA66,135 VII:274 Fsm A R	IX:243 IX:213 A F	XII:746 IX:242 :243 A A A				IX:213 F	IX:213 F			XII:668 Fm		IX:213 Fc
Unknown year and day	VIII:81 L	XI:270 F/A	XII:702 F/A	XII:703 F/A	XII:727 F/A																									
Unknown day	XII:395 CENSUS Fo	XII:44 BENJ F?	XII:50 BENJ Fs/t	XII:56 BENJ Fsm	IX:149 D-Y-L Am	VIII:60 Elam Lℓ	VIII:75 HABUR A	S143:132 =XVIII,p109 ADAD M. A	XII:547= IX:224 CENSUS F/A	RA 50 [TEM IV: viii] KAHAT Ap	M. DUSSAUD BENJ. Ap																			
Census II (#26b)																														

Zimri-Lim

	1	2	3	4	5	6	7	8	9	10	11	12	13	14	15
Euphrates (#29)		XVIII:50 A		XVIII:51 A/t											
Benjaminites (#6)	XI:29 Fsm	XII:58 Fsm	XII:59 Fsm		XII:60 Fsm				XII:61 Fc			XI:30 XII:62 F Fc			
Benjaminites II (#7)															
Ašlakka (#2)					XII:18 Fc										
Ašlakka II (#3)												[IX:237] Fc ↓			
Throne of Šamaš (#16)	XII:173 [IX:214] → Rk F	XII:174 Fc F	F	F	F	F	F	XII:175 IX:40= [IX:237] Fo Fc Fc	F	XII:176 VII:101 Fm F Ap	XII:177 Fm F	XI:66 XII:179 :178 Fc Fm Fc	XI:67 Fm F	F	F
Throne of Šamaš II (#17)															
Census (#26)	IX:99 XII:396 Fm Rk	XII:397 Fm	XI:170 Fm										XII:398 Fc	IX:101 A	XII:399 IX:101 Fc A
Dūr Yaḫdun-Lim (#28)	[IX:168] → F	F	VII:153 F F	IX:161 F F	F	IX:162 F F	F	IX:163 XI:218 VII:120 F Ap Fo	XII:522 F F	F	XII:523 XI:219 F F Fc	XII:524 Fo F	XII:525 F F	XII:526 F F	F
Ḫatta (#21)	[IX:216] → F	F	XII:295 :296 F F Fc	F	XII:297 F	F	XII:298 F F	XII:299 :300 F F Fp	XII:301 F F	F	F	XI:122 F	F	XI:123 F F	F F
Ḫatta II (#21b)															
Elam Expedition (#13)															
Addu of Maḫanum (#18)							XVIII:64 Ap								
Babylon (#11)												S 52:30 =XVIII p108 A			
Babylon II (#12)															
Throne of Dagan (#14)															
Throne of Dagan II (#15)															
IInd Ašlakka (#3b)															

	16	17	18	19	20	21	22	23	24	25	26	27	28	29	30
Euphrates (#29)															
Benjaminites (#6)				XI:31 F/t			XI:34 Fc			[VII:88] A					
Benjaminites II (#7)															
Ašlakka (#2)					XI:14 Fc	VII:86 A									
Ašlakka II (#3)															
Throne of Šamaš (#16)	XII:181 :182 F F Fo	XI:68 XII:183 XVIII:42 Fc A Fo	F	F	XII:184 Fo F	F	F	F	F	XII:185 Fo F	F	XII:186 :187 Fc F Fc	F	F	XII:188 → F F
Throne of Šamaš II (#17)															
Census (#26)	IX:101 A		XI:173 Fo	XI:171 Fm	IX:100 :102 Fm A	XII:400 Fo	IX:103 VII:133 Fm A			XII:401 Fo	IX:104 Fm	XII:403 R	XI:172 Fm		XI:174 Fm
Dūr Yaḫdun-Lim (#28)	F	F	XII:527 F F	XII:528 F F	XII:529 Fo F	F	F	XII:530 F F	XII:531 Fo F	XII:532 :533 F F Fo	IX:164 Fo F	IX:165 F F	XII:534 IX:165 :166 F Fo Fo	IX:167 F F	→ F
Ḫatta (#21)	XI:124 F/A	XII:302 F F	F →	Fc				XII:303 [IX:216] → Fc F	F	F	XII:304 F F	F	XI:125 F	F	XII:305 [IX:216] F
Ḫatta II (#21b)															
Elam Expedition (#13)															
Addu of Maḫanum (#18)									VIII:88 Ap/R						S 143:59 =XVIII p 109 A
Babylon (#11)															
Babylon II (#12)															
Throne of Dagan (#14)								IX:35 A							
Throne of Dagan II (#15)															
IInd Ašlakka (#3b)															

XII EBŪRUM (2)

Zimri-Lim

	1	2	3	4	5	6	7	8	9	10	11	12	13	14	15	16	17	18	19	20	21	22	23	24	25	26	27	28	29	30
Throne of his Father (#1)																														
Kaḫat (#4)			[SYRIA, 41 53 (=RA 66, 33)] A																											
Kaḫat II (#4b)																														
Mišlān (#5)																														
Elam Victory (#8)																														
Elaḫut Victory (#9)																														
Qarni-Lim (#10)																														
IInd Babylon (#12b)																														
Throne of Diritum (#19)																														
Addu of Halab (#20)																														
Annunitum of Šehrum (#22)																														
Addu of Appan (#23)																														
Addu of Appan II (#24)																														
Lions of Dagan (#25)																														
Šaramā (#27)																														
Ḫabur (#30)																														
Muballittum (#31)																														
Yamḫad (#32)																														

Zimri-Lim

	1	2	3	4	5	6	7	8	9	10	11	12	13	14	15	16	17	18	19	20	21	22	23	24	25	26	27	28	29	30
Andariq (#33!)								[VII:307 A ↓]																						
Unknown year	XII:724 [IX:215] → Fo F	XII:639 F F	XII:724 Fo F	F	VII:262 F F	F	F	XII:724 VII:210 :268 Fo A A	XII:724 Fo F	XI:258 F F	XII:724 IX:281 Fo F A	XII:724 Fo	VII:254 A	VII:209 :231 :232 Ap Ap Ap	F	VI:34 XIII:76 :77 E Etx Etx	F	F →	XI:258 Fm	XI:271 [IX:215] → Fc	F	XIII:78-80 → Etx			XIII:81 [IX:215] → Etx	F	F	F	F	F →
Unknown year and day	VII:210-212 Apt	[VIII:58] Lℓ	XII:641 Rk	XI:272 Fm	XII:640 Fm	XII:704 F/A	XII:709 F/A	XII:727 F/Fo	IX:222 F																					
Unknown day	VIII:37 ŠAMAŠ Lℓ	XII:403 CENSUS Fc	RA64,26 D-Y-L R	VII:123 [HATTA] Ap	XI:126 HATTA F	VIII:28 ADAD 9 Ap II Lℓ	XII:63 BENJ Rk	XII:547 ≃ IX:224 CENSUS F/A	VIII:49 ŠAMAŠ Lℓ	VIII:58 EUPHRATES c. Lℓ.																				
Census II (#26b)																														

V H̬IBIRTUM II (Intercalary) (1)

Zimri-Lim

	1	2	3	4	5	6	7	8	9	10	11	12	13	14	15	16	17	18	19	20	21	22	23	24	25	26	27	28	29	30
Euphrates (#29)																														
Benjaminites (#6)																														
Benjaminites II (#7)																														
Ašlakka (#2)																														
Ašlakka II (#3)																														
Throne of Šamaš (#16)																														
Throne of Šamaš II (#17)																														
Census (#26)																														
Dūr Yah̬dun-Lim (#28)																														
H̬atta (#21)																														
H̬atta II (#21b)																														
Elam Expedition (#13)																														
Addu of Mah̬anum (#18)																														
Babylon (#11)						SYRIA 55 p342 A																		IX:23 A						
Babylon II (#12)																														
Throne of Dagan (#14)																	S133:115 =XVIII p. 108-109 F													
Throne of Dagan II (#15)																														
IInd Ašlakka (#3b)																														

Zimri-Lim

	1	2	3	4	5	6	7	8	9	10	11	12	13	14	15	16	17	18	19	20	21	22	23	24	25	26	27	28	29	30
Throne of his Father (#1)																														
Kaḫat (#4)																														
Kaḫat II (#4b)																														
Mišlān (#5)																														
Elam Victory (#8)																														
Elaḫut Victory (#9)																														
Qarni-Lim (#10)																														
IInd Babylon (#12b)																														
Throne of Diritum (#19)																														
Addu of Halab (#20)																														
Annunitum of Šehrum (#22)																														
Addu of Appan (#23)																														
Addu of Appan II (#24)																														
Lions of Dagan (#25)																														
Šaramā (#27)																														
Ḫabur (#30)																														
Muballittum (#31)																														
Yamḫad (#32)																														

Zimri-Lim

	1	2	3	4	5	6	7	8	9	10	11	12	13	14	15	16	17	18	19	20	21	22	23	24	25	26	27	28	29	30
Andariq (#33!)																														
Unknown year								IX:236 Fc/t																						
Unknown year and day																														
Unknown day																														
Census II (#26b)																														

Zimri-Lim

	1	2	3	4	5	6	7	8	9	10	11	12	13	14	15	16	17	18	19	20	21	22	23	24	25	26	27	28	29	30
Euphrates (#29)																														
Benjaminites (#6)																				XII:64 Fsm	[XII:66?] Fsm		XII:65 Fsm	XI:33 Fsm	[VII:88] A					
Benjaminites II (#7)																														
Aškakka (#2)																														
Ašlakka II (#3)																														
Throne of Šamaš (#16)																														
Throne of Šamaš II (#17)																														
Census (#26)																														
Dūr Yaḫdun-Lim (#28)																														
Ḫatta (#21)																														
Ḫatta II (#21b)																														
Elam Expedition (#13)																														
Addu of Maḫanum (#18)																														
Babylon (#11)																														
Babylon II (#12)																														
Throne of Dagan (#14)																														
Throne of Dagan II (#15)																														
IInd Ašlakka (#3b)																														

Zimri-Lim	1	2	3	4	5	6	7	8	9	10	11	12	13	14	15	16	17	18	19	20	21	22	23	24	25	26	27	28	29	30
Throne of his Father (#1)																														
Kaḫat (#4)																														
Kaḫat II (#4b)																														
Mišlān (#5)																														
Elam Victory (#8)																														
Elaḫut Victory (#9)																														
Qarni-Lim (#10)																														
IInd Babylon (#12b)																														
Throne of Diritum (#19)																														
Addu of Halab (#20)																														
Annunitum of Šehrum (#22)																														
Addu of Appan (#23)																														
Addu of Appan II (#24)																														
Lions of Dagan (#25)																														
Šaramā (#27)																														
Ḫabur (#30)																														
Muballittum (#31)																														
Yamḫad (#32)																														

Zimri-Lim

	1	2	3	4	5	6	7	8	9	10	11	12	13	14	15	16	17	18	19	20	21	22	23	24	25	26	27	28	29	30
Andariq (#33!)																														
Unknown year																					XII:667 [BENJ.] Fsm									
Unknown year and day																														
Unknown day	XII:66 BENJ. Fsm	XII:67 BENJ. Fsm																												
Census II (#26b)																														

P/BIRIZARRU (TERQA) (2)

Zimri-Lim

	1	2	3	4	5	6	7	8	9	10	11	12	13	14	15	16	17	18	19	20	21	22	23	24	25	26	27	28	29	30
Throne of his Father (#1)																														
Kaḫat (#4)																														
Kaḫat II (#4b)																														
Mišlān (#5)																														
Elam Victory (#8)																														
Elaḫut Victory (#9)		IX:13 F/A																												
Qarni-Lim (#10)																														
IInd Babylon (#12b)																														
Throne of Diritum (#19)																														
Addu of Halab (#20)																														
Annunitum of Šehrum (#22)																														
Addu of Appan (#23)																														
Addu of Appan II (#24)																														
Lions of Dagan (#25)																														
Šaramā (#27)																														
Ḫabur (#30)																														
Muballiṭtum (#31)																														
Yamḫad (#32)																														

Zimri-Lim

	1	2	3	4	5	6	7	8	9	10	11	12	13	14	15	16	17	18	19	20	21	22	23	24	25	26	27	28	29	30
Andariq (#33!)																														
Unknown year																											IX:245 A			
Unknown year and day	IX:253 Ap																													
Unknown day																														
Census II (#26b)																														

ADNATUM (1)

Zimri-Lim	1	2	3	4	5	6	7	8	9	10	11	12	13	14	15	16	17	18	19	20	21	22	23	24	25	26	27	28	29	30
Euphrates (#29)																														
Benjaminites (#6)																														
Benjaminites II (#7)																														
Ašlakka (#2)										VIII:78 L																				
Ašlakka II (#3)																														
Throne of Šamaš (#16)																														
Throne of Šamaš II (#17)																														
Census (#26)																														
Dūr Yaḫdun-Lim (#28)																														
Ḫatta (#21)																														
Ḫatta II (#21b)																														
Elam Expedition (#13)																														
Addu of Maḫanum (#18)																														
Babylon (#11)																														
Babylon II (#12)																														
Throne of Dagan (#14)																														
Throne of Dagan II (#15)																														
IInd Ašlakka (#3b)																														